This short work, written by an influential philosopher of religion, shows how systematic theology is itself largely a philosophical enterprise. After analysing the nature of philosophical inquiry and its relation to systematic theology, and after exploring how theology requires that we talk about God, Vincent Brümmer illustrates how philosophical analysis can help in dealing with various conceptual problems involved in the fundamental Christian claim that God is a personal being with whom we may live in a personal relationship. Special attention is paid to the reason why theodicy arguments often appear insensitive to those who suffer, and therefore fail to offer them consolation, and in this connection the work of recent philosophers such as Richard Swinburne and D. Z. Phillips is evaluated and compared.

SPEAKING OF A PERSONAL GOD

SPEAKING OF A
PERSONAL GOD

An essay in philosophical theology

VINCENT BRÜMMER

Professor in the Philosophy of Religion, University of Utrecht

CAMBRIDGE
UNIVERSITY PRESS

Published by the Press Syndicate of the University of Cambridge
The Pitt Building, Trumpington Street, Cambridge CB2 1RP
40 West 20th Street, New York, NY 10011-4211, USA
10 Stamford Road, Oakleigh, Victoria 3166, Australia

First published 1992

Printed in Great Britain at the University Press, Cambridge

A catalogue record for this book is available from the British Library

Library of Congress cataloguing in publication data

Brümmer, Vincent.
Speaking of a personal God: an essay in philosophical theology /
Vincent Brümmer.
p.   cm.
Includes bibliographical references and index.
ISBN 0 521 43052 6 (hardback) – ISBN 0 521 43632 x (paperback)
1. God. 2. Philosophical theology. I. Title.
BT102. B75 1992
211 – dc20   92-3747   CIP

ISBN 0521 43052 6 hardback
ISBN 0521 43632 x paperback

Contents

Acknowledgements

In writing this book, I have made use of much material which has previously appeared in article form in Dutch or in English in various journals. I wish therefore to acknowledge the use I have been able to make of material taken from the following papers which I have written in the course of a number of years: 'Genade en onwederstandelijkheid' (with Professor C. Graafland), *Theologia Reformata*, 24 (1981); 'Over God gesproken', *Kerk en Theologie*, 33 (1982); 'Het kwaad en de goedheid van God', *Nederlands Theologisch Tijdschrift*, 36 (1982); 'Divine impeccability', *Religious Studies*, 20 (1984); 'Troost en theodicee', *Nederlands Theologisch Tijdschrift*, 41 (1987); 'Philosophical theology as conceptual recollection', *Neue Zeitschrift für Systematische Theologie und Religionsphilosophie*, 32 (1990); 'Farrer, Wiles and the causal joint', *Modern Theology*, 8 (1992). I would also like to thank the many colleagues who have helped me with criticisms of the ideas presented in these papers. Their comments and suggestions have enabled me to avoid many mistakes and in many ways to strengthen the arguments which I now put forward here. Last but not least, I would like to thank Gijsbert van den Brink and Marcel Sarot for their assistance and their many useful suggestions in preparing the final manuscript of this book.

CHAPTER I

Philosophical theology

I.I INTRODUCTION: PHILOSOPHY AND THEOLOGY

Between theologians and philosophers there has often been a strange love–hate relationship. On the one hand, philosophers have a fundamental interest in those features of human existence on which theologians reflect, while theologians are very much dependent on the methodological tools which philosophers provide. In fact, as we shall argue below, systematic theology can itself be interpreted as largely a philosophical enterprise. On the other hand, however, philosophers have often demanded that religious believers justify their truth claims by standards of rationality which these claims can never meet to the satisfaction of philosophers, and which many theologians consider to be quite inappropriate to the nature of the claims in question. In their view religious belief must be judged on its own terms and does not require any extraneous philosophical foundations or justifications. This opposition is well expressed by Anthony Kenny:

Some theologians regard religion as a way of life which can only be understood by participation and therefore cannot be justified to an outsider on neutral rational grounds. Such people must consider any attempt at a philosophical proof of God's existence to be wrong-headed... To me it seems that if belief in the existence of God cannot be rationally justified, there can be no good grounds for adopting any of the traditional monotheistic religions.[1]

In the view of many philosophers, then, theology is so obscurantist as to lack all intellectual respectability, whereas

[1] Anthony Kenny, *The Five Ways* (London, 1968), 4.

many theologians have a deep distrust of philosophers whose intolerable demands are aimed at undermining the faith. The result is that the very term 'philosophical theology' seems to many philosophers and theologians to be a contradiction in terms!

This estrangement between philosophy and theology has been aggravated by a prejudice dating from the Enlightenment, that epistemological issues are central to all intellectual inquiry. The basic issue is that of finding an epistemological justification for the claims which are made. The primary question to be faced is: 'How do you know?', and philosophers and theologians seem to differ with respect to the answers they consider appropriate and adequate.[2] Much recent work in philosophical theology breaks this stalemate by following Wittgenstein in 'a refusal to make philosophy the provider of foundations and justifications'.[3] The task of philosophical theology is not to provide proofs of the truth (or falsity) of the Christian faith, or to find neutral rational grounds on which to justify accepting (or rejecting) the Christian, or any other faith. Instead the philosophical theologian asks semantic and hermeneutical questions about the meaning and interpretation of the faith: what are the implications and presuppositions of the fundamental concepts of the faith, and how could the claims of the faith be interpreted in a coherent and relevant way? In this sense philosophical theology has an essential contribution to make in the theological quest of faith seeking understanding.

In this book I will try to explain this view about the task of philosophical theology, and to illustrate it with an inquiry into the implications and presuppositions of one of the central claims

---

[2] Usually these answers presuppose some version of 'foundationalism'. For criticism of the foundationalist paradigm, see, for example, N. Wolterstorff, *Reason within the Bounds of Religion* (Grand Rapids, MI, 1976), 24ff, A. Plantinga, 'Reason and belief in God', in Plantinga and Wolterstorff (eds.), *Faith and Rationality* (Notre Dame, IN, 1983), 16–93, D. Z. Phillips, *Faith after Foundationalism* (London, 1988), and from a non-religious point of view, Richard Rorty, *Philosophy and the Mirror of Nature* (Princeton, NJ, 1979) and Richard J. Bernstein, *Beyond Objectivism and Relativism* (Oxford, 1983).

[3] D. Z. Phillips, *Belief, Change and Forms of Life* (London, 1986), 3. See also Norman Malcolm, 'The groundlessness of belief', in Malcolm, *Thought and Knowledge* (Ithaca, NY, 1977), 199–216.

of the Christian faith, namely that God is a personal being with whom we may live in a personal relation. The first two chapters will deal with the methodological issues regarding the relation between theology and philosophical inquiry, while chapters 3 to 6 will be devoted to an analysis of the concept of a personal God.

In the present chapter I will discuss the nature of philosophical theology and the way it is related to hermeneutics and to confessional theology or dogmatics. Chapter 2 will deal with a basic presupposition of philosophical theology, namely that coherent theo-logy or God-talk is possible. In an important sense this presupposition is sometimes questioned by theologians on the grounds that God is the 'Wholly Other' who transcends the field of application of all our human concepts. All attempts at saying something about God can only be negative or dialectical or paradoxical. The demand of philosophical theology that we should interpret the claims of the faith in a logically coherent way is therefore illegitimate. I will argue that, although this attitude to philosophical theology is both misguided and self-defeating, it does point towards the essentially metaphorical nature of religious thought as something which philosophical theology should take seriously.

The second half of the book will illustrate this view on the nature of philosophical theology by means of an extended analysis of some key aspects of the religious claim that we as human persons can live our lives in a personal relationship with God. This claim presupposes that both we and God are persons in relation to each other. This in turn entails that both God and human persons are free agents in relation to each other. Does this mean that we are free and able to resist the grace of God and that God is free and able to do evil in relation to us? These two questions will be discussed in chapters 3 and 4 respectively. Chapter 5 will deal with the relation between divine and human agency, and especially the so-called doctrine of double agency according to which God can act through the things that human agents do. It is clear that the issues raised in this discussion of divine and human freedom and agency have important implications for the traditional problem of theodicy: how can evil and suffering be reconciled with the love of God? Chapter 6 discusses the nature of this question and the way in which it has usually been answered in the Christian tradition. Special attention will be paid to the reasons why theodicy arguments often appear morally insensitive to those who suffer and therefore fail to offer them any consolation.

In an epilogue, I will summarize briefly what light our reflections on talk of a personal God throw on the issues raised at the beginning regarding the relationship between theology and philosophical inquiry. I will argue that, although reaching theological conclusions requires more than philosophical reflection, systematic theology is unable to deal with theological issues like those discussed in this book without implicitly or explicitly making use of the tools of the philosopher. In the end, systematic theology remains to a large extent a philosophical enterprise.

1.2 CONCEPTUAL RECOLLECTION

When the first grammar book of the Castilian language was presented to Queen Isabella of Castile, her response was to ask what use it was to fluent speakers of Castilian, since it told them nothing that they did not know already. Although in a sense it was true that they knew the grammar of their language, there was another sense in which they did not know it. Their intuitive ability to construct grammatically correct Castilian sentences showed that they effortlessly observed a system of grammatical rules. But from this it by no means follows that they could effortlessly or with an effort say what these rules were. The ability to do something correctly, in this case speak grammatically, is very different from and does not necessarily involve the ability to say how it should be done. P. F. Strawson uses this example[4] to illustrate how philosophical inquiry is aimed at finding out things which we know all along. Thus people are able to think and to argue logically even when they have never heard of logic. In reply to a remark like that of Queen Isabella, one could point out that this sort of philosophical inquiry has a

[4] P. F. Strawson, 'Different conceptions of analytical philosophy', *Tijdschrift voor Filosofie*, 35 (1973), 803.

twofold use. On the one hand, it has a constructive use in supplying explicit insight into thought forms which we would otherwise only master intuitively. On the other hand, it also has a therapeutic use in helping us to sort out conceptual dilemmas and logical mistakes in our thinking. Let us examine the nature of this kind of philosophical reflection on the forms of thought with which we are in a sense already familiar. After examining the form this reflection takes with such diverse philosophers as Plato, the followers of Wittgenstein and Hans-Georg Gadamer, and the implications which this has for the way philosophers read texts, we will try in the following sections of this chapter to determine whose thought forms are the object of philosophical reflection, and whether this kind of reflection is innovative or merely descriptive. In conclusion we will see what this implies for the nature of philosophical theology as a reflection on the faith, and how this is related to the kind of reflection characteristic of confessional theology or dogmatics.

It is of course not a new idea that philosophy tries to find out things which we all know all along. Thus Plato let Meno ask of Socrates:

But in what way, Socrates, will you search for a thing of which you are entirely ignorant? For by what mark which may discover it will you look for it when you know none of the marks that distinguish it? Or, if you should not fail of meeting with it, how will you discern it, when met with, to be the very thing you were in search of, and knew nothing of before?[5]

Plato tried to solve this puzzle by means of his view that philosophy is a kind of recollection (anamnesis): the philosopher tries to recall the vision of the ideas which his soul enjoyed during its pre-existence in the realm of ideas, and which has now been blurred on account of the soul being incarcerated in a body. For our purposes three questions are important with respect to this platonic theory: What is the nature of concepts? How does recollection take place? In what sense does this recollection lead to progress in our thought?

For Plato concepts are memory images of the ideas. In our

---

[5] Plato, *Meno* 80d.

bodily state these memories have become so vague that we have to make a special effort to recall them. This kind of *conceptual recollection* is a task for philosophers. How does this take place? Since for Plato the world of sense experience has been fashioned as an imperfect copy of the ideas, it can serve as a mnemonic to remind us of the ideas. For this reason the platonic philosopher is the very opposite of Rodin's *Le Penseur* who sits contemplating with his eyes closed. Platonic recollection is done with your eyes open, looking at the world in order to be reminded of the ideas. It follows that there are two ways of looking at the empirical world. We can look at the world either in order to learn something about *it*, or in order to be reminded of the *ideas*. In the first case we extend our knowledge of the world of experience. In the second case we extend our explicit knowledge of the ideas and in this way become explicitly aware of our concepts as mental representations of the ideas.

Progress in philosophy consists in extending our explicit knowledge of the eternal ideas. The philosopher achieves this to the extent that he manages to form ideal concepts in the sense of perfect mental representations of the ideas. In this way philosophy aims at extending our insight into essentially immutable objects. This has a constructive purpose in extending our insight into the eternal ideas, as well as a therapeutic value in helping us to improve our conceptual forms in the direction of the eternal ideal.

In an interesting essay[6] R. M. Hare also defends the view that philosophy could be described as a kind of recollection. However, in doing so he tries to demythologize the platonic theory along more or less Wittgensteinian lines. Hare explains his view with the help of the following example:

Suppose that we are sitting at dinner and discussing how a certain dance is danced. Let us suppose that the dance in question is one requiring the participation of a number of people – say one of the Scottish reels. And let us suppose that we have a dispute about what happens at a particular point in the dance; and that, in order to settle it, we decide to dance the dance after dinner and find out. We have to

[6] R. M. Hare, 'Philosophical discoveries', in Hare, *Essays on Philosophical Method* (London, 1971), 19ff.

imagine that there is among us a sufficiency of people who know, or say they know, how to dance the dance – in the sense of 'know' in which one may know how to do something without being able to *say* how it is done.[7]

Interpreting conceptual recollection on the analogy of this example suggests a number of significant differences from Plato's theory.

The first important difference concerns the nature of concepts. Here concepts are no longer seen as mental representations but rather as mental capacities, that is, capacities to perform certain mental activities.[8] Thus the concept of red is not a mental representation of redness, but the ability to distinguish things that are red from things that are not; the concept of 'I' is the ability to distinguish myself from everything else; the concept of identity is the ability to see when one thing is the same as another; and the concept of negation is the ability to see when one thing is not the same as another. Since we usually use language in exercising these capacities, it can also be said that someone has mastered a concept if he is able to use the relevant word or expression or construction correctly. In the words of Peter Geach:

It will be a *sufficient* condition for James's having the concept of *so-and-so* that he should have mastered the intelligent use (including the use in made-up sentences) of a word for *so-and-so* in some language. Thus: if somebody knows how to use the English word 'red', he has a concept of red; if he knows how to use the first-person pronoun, he has a concept of *self*; if he knows how to use the negative construction in some language, he has a concept of negation.[9]

Furthermore, thinking and talking resemble dancing not only in being activities, but also in being rule-guided. Hence conceptual recollection is aimed not merely at recalling how these activities are performed, but also at how they should be performed. In Hare's example the dancers tried to recall the rules which they were able to apply intuitively when dancing. Similarly, in Strawson's example, the Castilian grammarians

---

[7] Ibid., 22.
[8] For a more detailed comparison between these two views on the nature of concepts, see chapter 3 of my *Theology and Philosophical Inquiry* (London, 1981).
[9] Peter Geach, *Mental Acts* (London, 1957), 12.

were recalling the grammatical rules which Castilians were able to apply intuitively when talking Castilian, and logicians try to recall the rules which we all apply intuitively when arguing logically. In this sense philosophical reflection is aimed at recalling the rules which constitute the exercise of our conceptual capacities.

A further significant difference between the views of Hare and Plato on the nature of concepts has to do with their origin. While Plato supposed that as philosophers we are trying to remember something we learned in a former life, Hare argues that 'what we are actually remembering is what we learned on our mothers' knees, and cannot remember learning'.[10] Our conceptual forms are not acquired through experience in some pre-existent state, but through the process of socialization by which we inherit all aspects of our culture. This in turn implies that concepts do not represent timeless essential forms, but are in fact aspects of our culture which are in principle subject to historical change and cultural variation.

Like that of Plato, Hare's kind of recollection is performed with open eyes. In this he follows the Wittgensteinian injunction: 'Don't think. Look!' In trying to recall how a certain activity should be performed, we look at the way in which people in fact perform it. Thus we are reminded of the way the dance should be danced by looking at the way it is in fact done, and we are reminded of the way in which our conceptual capacities should be exercised by looking at the way people use words in order to exercise them. Here ordinary language usage functions as mnemonic for philosophical recollection. As with Plato, we can here also distinguish two ways of looking: in order to see what is being done and in order to recollect how it should be done. Hare[11] explains this distinction by comparing the way the dancers in his example look at the performance of the dance in order to be reminded of the rules according to which the dance should be danced, with the way a cultural anthropologist observes a dance in some primitive tribe in order to give an empirical description of how the dance is done. The anthro-

---

[10] Hare, 'Philosophical discoveries', 37.   [11] Ibid., 25ff.

pologist describes how a particular dance is in fact being performed by a specific group of dancers on a specific occasion, while the dancers are trying to recollect how it should be danced correctly on all occasions. The dancers' recollection presupposes that they know how to dance the dance and are able to recognize a correct performance when they see it. The anthropologist's description does not necessarily presuppose that he or she has these abilities. Similarly, we could distinguish two ways of looking at ordinary language: in order to give an empirical description of the way people talk in fact, and in order to recollect the way conceptual skills should be exercised correctly. Thus, although philosophers do reflect on empirical data, their reflection is aimed at recollection and not at an empirical description of the data. Hare points out that 'this perhaps explains the odd fact that analytical enquiries seem often to start by collecting empirical data about word-uses, but to end with apparently *a priori* conclusions'.[12]

The difference between Hare and Plato on the nature of concepts entails a difference not only about the nature of philosophical recollection, but also about the nature of progress in philosophy. If our concepts do not represent timeless essential forms, as Plato held, but are aspects of our culture which are in principle subject to historical change and cultural variation, then progress in philosophy is not limited to the extension of our explicit insight into the structure of our thinking. The philosopher can also participate in the cultural process by suggesting possible ways of improving our conceptual forms. Thus Hare points out[13] that his dancers do not merely try to recollect the rules constituting the way the dance has always been performed. They also practise 'innovative dancing' in which suggestions are made for changing the rules. Philosophy does not necessarily leave anything the way it is, but can also generate improvements in our thinking. In section 1.3 below we will have to investigate what is to count as an improvement.

Hans-Georg Gadamer is a very different kind of philosopher from Plato and Hare. Nevertheless, many of the points raised

---

[12] Ibid., 32.   [13] Ibid., 33.

above with reference to Plato and Hare are also characteristic of
Gadamer's thinking. Without denying the differences, I would
like to point out the similarities, since these are instructive for
the view of philosophy as conceptual recollection.

In many respects Gadamer's hermeneutical theory[14] can be
seen as a reaction to the views of Schleiermacher and Dilthey.
According to these two thinkers the aim of textual interpretation
is to reproduce as accurately as possible the intention of the
author of the text. This is only possible if we interpret what the
author says in the light of the historical and cultural situation
and the conceptual presuppositions of the author. Hence we can
only recover the meaning of the text (i.e. the authorial intention)
by means of a disciplined reconstruction of the historical context
in which it originated. In order to achieve this, interpreters have
to eliminate the conceptual presuppositions and prejudices of
their own cultural and historical situation and adopt those of
the author whose text they are interpreting. In this way they
have to negate the temporal distance between themselves and
the author and imaginatively become contemporaneous with
the latter. It is clear that for Schleiermacher and Dilthey the
interpreter's own historical situation can only have a negative
value in the process of interpretation. It is the source of the
interpreter's own historical prejudices and distortions, which
block a clear understanding of the intentional meaning of the
text. For this reason hermeneutics requires that interpreters
should systematically neglect their own historicity.

Gadamer directs his criticism against this methodical alienation of interpreters from their own historicity, since for him this
not only entails a mistaken view concerning the role of the
interpreter and the nature of the interpretative enterprise, but
also overlooks the significance of the interpreter's prejudices.
The interpreter is reduced to the essentially situationless and
non-historical subject of neo-Kantian transcendental philo-

---

[14] For Gadamer's views, see his *Wahrheit und Methode: Grundzüge einer philosophischen
Hermeneutik* (Tübingen, 1960), English translation: *Truth and Method* (London,
1975), and Gadamer, *Philosophical Hermeneutics*, translated and edited by David E.
Linge (Berkeley, CA, 1977). Linge's introduction to the latter volume provides an
excellent summary of Gadamer's theory.

sophy, and the interpretative enterprise becomes an attempt at reproducing a past intention rather than a productive procedure involving the interpreter's own hermeneutical situation. Fundamental to these mistakes, however, is the view that the interpreter's conceptual prejudices are (a) to be eliminated from the interpretative process since (b) they form a barrier between the interpreter and the past tradition which is expressed in the text. Gadamer rejects both these points.

Our prejudices are essential to our understanding of the world and therefore cannot be eliminated. 'The historicity of our existence entails that prejudices, in the literal sense of the word, constitute the initial directedness of our whole ability to experience. Prejudices are the biases of our openness to the world.'[15] In fact our prejudices constitute our *horizon of understanding*, that is, the intuitive conceptual capacities in terms of which we understand the world. Understanding would become impossible if we were to eliminate these capacities and turn our minds into a blank, a *tabula rasa*. Furthermore, far from being a barrier between us and the past, these conceptual prejudices are the effects of the past on our present way of thinking and hence they provide our link with the tradition we are trying to understand. In other words, the intuitive conceptual capacities that constitute our horizon of understanding are inherited by us through the process of socialization which links us with the cultural tradition. As Hare would say: we have learned them on our mothers' knees. Hence we do not come to know the past by eliminating these conceptual prejudices that constitute our horizon of understanding, but precisely by trying to achieve an explicit awareness of them. In this sense it could therefore be said that for Gadamer, as for Plato and Hare, philosophical reflection can be described as a form of conceptual recollection. Gadamer's hermeneutics is aimed at recollecting the implicit conceptual capacities that constitute the horizon of understanding which we have inherited from the past.

For Gadamer too, this kind of conceptual recollection is performed with open eyes:

---

[15] Gadamer, *Philosophical Hermeneutics*, 9. See also *Wahrheit und Methode*, 261.

It is precisely in confronting the otherness of the text – in hearing its challenging viewpoint – and not in preliminary methodological self-purgations, that the reader's own prejudices (i.e., his present horizons) are thrown into relief and thus come to critical self-conscious-ness... Collision with the other's horizons makes us aware of assump-tions so deep-seated that they would otherwise remain unnoticed.[16]

For Gadamer the role of mnemonic is fulfilled by the texts, and conceptual recollection takes place in the 'hermeneutical conversation' between the interpreter and the text.

As was the case with both Plato and Hare, we can distinguish here too between two ways of looking: with a view to description and with a view to recollection. Thus we can look at a text in the way recommended by Schleiermacher and Dilthey, in order to reconstruct and describe the original intention of the author. Or, in the way recommended by Gadamer, we can look at a text as the author's actualization of the tradition, in order to recollect the intuitive conceptual prejudices which link us as interpreters with the tradition. In this way the tradition is actualized anew in the present. Gadamer describes this process of actualization by means of the metaphor of a game. If the game is played well, the individual players enter into the spirit of the game and become absorbed in it. In the end the real subject of playing is the game itself, and all playing is a being-played. Similarly, interpretation and understanding are move-ments within the *Wirkungsgeschichte* of the tradition. In the end it is the tradition which actualizes itself in the hermeneutical dialogue between the text and the interpreter.

As the term *Wirkungsgeschichte* suggests, our conceptual forms are not timeless and unchanging but involved in the ongoing historical process of the tradition. The hermeneutical dialogue between the interpreter and the text is therefore a creative process which brings forth something new, and does not merely reproduce what was there before. On the one hand, interpreting the text does not merely reproduce the author's intention but actualizes new possibilities from the 'excess of meaning' contained in the text and transcending the author's intention. Nor, on the other hand, does interpretation merely reproduce

[16] Linge, Introduction to Gadamer's *Philosophical Hermeneutics*, xxi.

the interpreter's horizon. The latter is modified by being confronted with the strange horizon of the text. In the hermeneutical process the horizons of the text and the interpreter are therefore fused in order to produce something new in which the tradition is transformed and progresses. Hence for Gadamer, as for Hare, conceptual recollection does not leave everything as it is, but creatively leads to progress in our conceptual forms. here, again, the problem is: What counts as progress? We shall return to this in section 1.3 below.

The customary way of identifying the meaning of a text with the author's intention has an obvious advantage: it enables us to maintain that there is only one canonical interpretation. The author intended something specific, and interpretation recovers the original intention while rejecting all competing interpretations as incorrect. Although there may be various explications of the *significance* of the text for us, it has only one *meaning*, and that is the meaning intended by the author. According to Gadamer, this distinction between meaning and significance cannot be maintained in the light of the history of interpretation. The interpreters of Plato, Aristotle, the Bible, and so on in various historical periods differed in *the meaning they thought they saw* in the text and not merely in their *views on the significance* that the same textual meaning had for each of them. Furthermore, for Gadamer the variety of interpretations cannot be reduced to mere subjective differences between the interpreters. It belongs to the ontological possibility of a text that it is ever open to new comprehensions. Since every text has an excess of meaning in the sense that it allows for a number of *natural* (i.e. non-contrived) interpretations, there is no reason to declare the *intentional* interpretation canonical. Most important, however, to do so would make understanding into a transaction between the creative consciousness of the author and the purely reproductive consciousness of the interpreter, and therefore fail to account for the creative role of interpretation in constituting the tradition.

On the one hand, Gadamer is correct in emphasizing the fact that every text has an 'excess of meaning' beyond the implicit or explicit intentions of the author. There are of course limits to the possible interpretations which are natural to the text: you cannot make a text say just anything you please without becoming contrived or sinning against the principle of descriptive caution.[17] Nevertheless, it remains an 'intentionalist fallacy' to claim that the intentional interpretation is the only one which is legitimate. As Denis Nineham remarks with reference to biblical interpretation: 'The modern reader can find in the Bible meaning in abundance, much of which the original authors could not possibly have envisaged in the quite different cultural circumstances of their times.'[18] Which interpretation we are to choose depends very much on our purpose in reading the text.[19] If we are historians who try to explain why the author said what he said, or how the author influenced and was influenced by the circumstances of his time, we will obviously go for the *intentional interpretation* of the text. If however we are philosophers aiming at 'conceptual recollection', we will probably choose the most *rational interpretation*, that is, the one that produces the most fruitful conceptual suggestions relevant to our own present situation.

On the other hand, Gadamer is unnecessarily negative in the view he takes of intentional interpretation. Apart from playing down the importance of such interpretations, he sometimes seems to suggest that they are in fact impossible. If, as Gadamer claims, it is impossible to exclude our own horizon of understanding when reading a text, then it becomes very difficult, if not impossible, to achieve the imaginative identification with the horizon of the author which is often claimed to be essential for achieving an intentional interpretation. However, the situation is not as bleak as this would suggest. Intentional interpretation of a text does not require us to *adopt* the horizon

---

[17] See F. R. Heeger, *Ideologie und Macht* (Uppsala, 1975), 11–12.

[18] Denis Nineham, *The Use and Abuse of the Bible* (London, 1976), 29.

[19] C. M. Wood makes a similar point: 'What it means to understand a text varies a great deal with one's aims. Historical understanding, literary understanding, and theological understanding (to mention three possibilities) are not identical.' 'Theological hermeneutics', *Quarterly Review*, 7 (1987), 99. For a more extended discussion, see also his book on *The Formation of Christian Understanding: An Essay in Theological Hermeneutics* (Philadelphia, PA, 1981). See also my paper on 'Philosophy, theology and the reading of texts', *Religious Studies*, 27 (1991), 451–62 for a comparison of the ways in which philosophers and theologians read texts.

of the author, but merely to *reconstruct* it in the light of the historical and cultural context in which the text was written. Interpreting a text in the light of the presuppositions and assumptions of the author does not require us to agree with these or to make them our own in any way. All we need to do is to find out what these presuppositions and assumptions were. It is usually possible to achieve this with reasonable accuracy by means of the procedure known as the 'hermeneutical circle',[20] provided we have some knowledge of the context in which the text was written.

Intentional interpretations are not only *possible*, but also *important*. Not only are they essential for historical research, but they have an important contribution to make as well in the process of philosophical hermeneutics aimed at conceptual recollection. As Gadamer correctly states, philosophical hermeneutics is aimed at achieving a 'fusion of horizons' in which the horizons of both the text and the interpreter are transformed, and something new is produced. This fails if on the one hand we limit ourselves to seeking an intentional interpretation which limits the horizon of the text to that of the author, and on the other hand, if we interpret the text in the light of our own horizon in such a way that our own conceptual presuppositions are merely confirmed and not changed. A philosophical interpretation of a text 'must insist on putting distance between the interpreter and the text so that the text is free to do more than merely mirror the beliefs and prejudices of the interpreter. It must be able to create the situation in which the interpreter occasionally may "not like" what he/she sees and learns.'[21] Intentional interpretation has a contribution to make to philosophical hermeneutics, since it is an important way of distancing the text from the biases of the interpreter. It is,

---

[20] 'The procedure must be to begin by interpreting the words on the basis of the best guesses we can make as to the original assumptions and presuppositions. In the light of the interpretation which that yields we may hope to refine our understanding of the presuppositions and then re-read the text on the basis of our new understanding of its assumptions. The process may have to be repeated many times and it may seem circular – it is in fact often referred to as the "hermeneutical circle".' Nineham, *The Use and Abuse of the Bible*, 26.

[21] Willard M. Swartley, *Slavery, Sabbath, War and Women* (Scottdale, PA, 1983), 219.

however, not the only, let alone the exclusive way in which this might be achieved. The philosophical interpreter should confront his or her own conceptual prejudices not only with those of the author of a text, but also with those of other interpreters. Swartley argues that, 'as interpreters listen to and learn from other interpreters – men from women, whites from blacks, western Christians from eastern Christians, the wealthy from the poor (and vice versa) – new discoveries of truth in both the text and the self will emerge'.[22] In brief, then, although intentional interpretation can make an important contribution to philosophical hermeneutics, Gadamer is correct in maintaining that this is not the primary (let alone the exclusive) aim of a philosophical reading of a text. The latter is aimed not at reconstructing the intentions of the author but at mediating in the present the conceptual tradition in which the interpreter participates by means of his or her own conceptual prejudices.

The philosopher looks at the world of experience (Plato), or at ordinary language usage (Hare) or at texts (Gadamer) in order to achieve conceptual 'recollection'. It is important to note, however, that in all this 'recollection' functions as a metaphor and, like all metaphors, it has its limitations. We have tried to show that it can serve very well to highlight some important features of philosophical reflection. However, it breaks down at other important points where philosophical reflection seems unlike recollection. Two of these are the following. As we ordinarily use the term 'recollection', it applies only to the memories of the person doing the recollecting. I can only recall my own memories and not those of somebody else. Do philosophers only reflect upon their own personal conceptual forms? Whose concepts are the object of philosophical reflections? Secondly, recollection is a 'conservative' term, in the sense that it is aimed at *recalling* memories and not at *creating* or *changing* them. We have argued above, however, that philosophical reflection is creative and innovative. At these two points we may have to 'stretch' the metaphor in order to apply it to philosophical reflection. In the two sections that follow, we

[22] Ibid., 220.

shall try to establish whose concepts are the object of philosophical 'recollection' and to what extent philosophical 'recollection' can be innovative and not merely descriptive.

1.3 CONCEPTUAL IMAGINATION

If in philosophy we try to recollect 'our' conceptual prejudices,
whom do we include among 'us'? Whose concepts are the
object of our philosophical reflection? If, like Plato, we were to
hold that philosophical reflection is aimed at recollecting the
unchanging essential meaning of concepts, then we are looking
for something which is universally the same for all people in all
times. In that case the 'we' of philosophers necessarily includes
everybody. We have argued above that this view mistakenly
denies the historicity of human thought. Human concepts are
not timelessly the same, but subject to both synchronic
variations across cultures and diachronic change through
history. Hence all 'our' concepts are not necessarily shared by
everybody and the question arises as to whose concepts we are
to reflect upon.

A possible alternative would be to limit our attention to the
conceptual forms of a specific culture or period in the history of
thought. In that case philosophy would become a descriptive
discipline: either a kind of cultural anthropology of human
thought which describes the conceptual forms current in a
specific cultural environment, or a kind of cultural histori-
ography of human thought which describes the conceptual
forms current in a specific historical period. It is true that
philosophers sometimes pursue this sort of inquiry. Maybe this
is what the joker had in mind who accused Heidegger of
'turning the idiosyncrasies of the German language into
philosophy'! And did not British linguistic analysis sometimes
tend to become an attempt at describing the conceptual forms
inherent in the English language? Even if we admit that this sort
of conceptual description is an academically respectable enterprise, it is nevertheless not philosophy in the sense of the
conceptual recollection we described above. This descriptive
activity is analogous to Hare's cultural anthropologist de-

scribing the way the primitives are dancing, rather than to Hare's dancers trying to recollect how the dance should be performed.

We might also take the metaphor of 'recollection' at its face value and admit that in the end every philosopher is trying to recollect his own individual thought forms, as he learned these 'on his mother's knee' or as he inherited them as an individual from the cultural tradition in which he stands. Was Plato's philosopher not trying to recollect his own antenatal vision of the ideas, and Hare's dancers their own intuitive knowledge of how to perform the dance? And does not Gadamer's emphasis on the 'reflexive dimension' of interpretation entail that interpreters try to recollect their own implicit prejudices? And is Stanley Cavell[23] not somehow correct in his suggestion that Wittgenstein's *Philosophical Investigations* belongs to the genre of the Confession?

True as this suggestion might be, it is not the whole truth. Philosophical reflection can never be a purely solipsistic affair because human thought, like human language and human culture, necessarily presupposes intersubjectivity. Therefore philosophers claim to go beyond subjectivism: my conceptual recollections are also valid for you whenever my concepts are common to both of us. Since I share my horizon of understanding with others, my philosophical conclusions are claimed to refer to 'us' and not only to 'me'. However, this merely brings us back to the question with which we started: Where are the limits of the commonality of our own concepts? And what gives me the right to claim that my conceptual recollections are to be shared by others?

What Stanley Cavell says of Wittgenstein might be helpful at this point. Cavell points out that Wittgenstein was well aware of the fact that his claims about 'what we say' were not necessarily shared by everybody. Hence his attempts to 'say what we say' should not be interpreted as generalizations from 'I say' to 'we say' but rather as invitations to others to see whether they could share his conceptual recollections. 'We may think of it as a

---

[23] Stanley Cavell, *The Claim of Reason: Wittgenstein, Scepticism, Morality, and Tragedy* (Oxford, 1979), 20.

sample. The introduction of the sample by the words "We say..." is an invitation for you to see whether you have such a sample, or can accept mine as a sound one.'[24] Such invitations are not a priori claims to conceptual community, but rather attempts to find the basis for such community, and 'the wish and search for community are the wish and search for reason'.[25]

Although there is much to be said for this view, it is in one sense too restrictive. The 'samples' that philosophers invite others to consider are not derived solely from their own personal conceptual prejudices. As D. Z. Phillips shows, 'people do not restrict their philosophizings to themes and concepts for which they have a use when not philosophizing'. Thus, for example, 'philosophers who stand in no personal relationship to religion may still philosophize about it'.[26] In brief, philosophical reflection is not an ego-trip; not even an ego-trip in which the philosopher tries to involve other people!

Perhaps we should rather say that philosophers reflect on *possible* conceptual forms and not merely on their own *actual* concepts. The latter form only a small part of the possibilities to be considered. The form of a philosophical problem is not: 'Is this the way I think?' nor: 'Can you share this sample from my conceptual horizon?' but rather: 'Imagine what it would be like if we thought thus...' In this way the Socratic dialogues dealt with such problems as: 'Imagine what it would be like if knowing were the same as perceiving', or: 'Imagine what it would be like if piety were the same as being approved by the gods.' And Wittgenstein's *Philosophical Investigations* abounds with passages introduced by the words: '(Let us) imagine...' Hence philosophical reflection is not merely an exercise in recollection, but also, as Husserl tells us, an exercise in imagination. However, recollections cannot be eliminated either. The only reason for considering imaginary conceptual forms is to see whether or not or to what extent they are to be preferred to the ones we can recollect. Similarly, Gadamer might say that the only reason interpreters consider the strange horizon of the text is to see whether or not or to what extent it

---

[24] Ibid., 19.   [25] Ibid., 20.   [26] Phillips, *Belief, Change and Forms of Life*, 43.

is to be preferred to their own. Adapting Gadamer's term, we could say that philosophical reflection aims at a 'fusion' of imagination and recollection. Clearly this conclusion implies that philosophical reflection is not merely descriptive but also innovative, producing conceptual forms which are to be *preferred* to those with which we are familiar. This leads us to the other major issue raised in section 1.2 above: What criteria do we have for deciding which conceptual forms are to be 'preferred', or are to count as innovations which improve our way of thinking?

1.4 CONCEPTUAL INNOVATION

Changes in the circumstances and demands of life bring about changes in culture and hence also in the conceptual forms that people find adequate, including the concomitant beliefs that they hold to be true. 'A statement whose truth or falsity can be determined only in terms of a world-view that is dead and gone can hardly be a statement of direct relevance to subsequent ages; old formulas...conceived in another intellectual atmosphere no longer say what needs to be said or no longer say it suitably.'[27] The more we become aware of the cultural differences between various times and places, the more we come to realize the untenability of the platonic claim that human thought is essentially immutable. Because of changes in the demands of life, our conceptual forms cannot remain eternally adequate. According to Wittgenstein,

earlier physicists are said to have found suddenly that they had too little mathematical understanding to cope with physics; and in almost the same way young people today can be said to be in a situation where ordinary common sense no longer suffices to meet the strange demands life makes. Everything has become so intricate that mastering it would require an exceptional intellect. Because skill at playing the game is no longer enough, the question that keeps coming up is: can this game be played at all now and what would be the right game to play?[28]

[27] Maurice Wiles, *The Making of Christian Doctrine* (Cambridge, 1967), 9.
[28] Ludwig Wittgenstein, *Culture and Value* (Oxford, 1980), 27e. See also Phillips, *Belief, Change and Forms of Life*, 49.

This has profound implications for the nature of philosophical reflection. It is not enough for the philosopher merely to try to 'recollect' the rules which constitute our conceptual games. He or she must also inquire whether these conceptual games are still adequate 'to meet the strange demands life makes' and whether innovations are not called for in order to make them so. Philosophy cannot remain purely descriptive. It is required to be innovative as well.

There are, however, limits to the possibility of innovation. These have to do with the point we raised in the previous section: thought, like language and culture, presupposes intersubjectivity. Our conceptual games are co-operative activities which are only possible in community. Conceptual innovations which are too far removed from the conceptual forms which are familiar to the community, become unrecognizable for others and thus make co-operation impossible. Hare explains this with reference to speaking and dancing:

What makes co-operation possible in both these activities is that the speaker or dancer should not do things which make the other people say 'We don't know what to make of this'. That is to say, he must not do things which cannot be easily related to the unformulated rules of speaking or dancing which everybody knows who has learned to perform these activities.[29]

The consequence of this limitation is that philosophers who suggest conceptual innovations must necessarily leave the greater part of the conceptual status quo unchallenged and unchanged. Thus Denis Nineham points out that

we can see all this if we consider the achievements of men who are generally regarded as having been responsible for major changes of outlook, men like Mohammed, Martin Luther or Karl Marx. It implies no underestimation of their real achievements to insist that what they left unchallenged in the presuppositions of their times was far, far more than anything they challenged or changed. From our perspective the chief impression made by Luther, for example, is that of a late medieval theologian, while Karl Marx strikes us as in many ways a typical middle-class nineteenth-century German intellectual who took over unquestioned a great deal of Hegel's philosophy and a

[29] Hare, 'Philosophical discoveries', 33.

lot more of the generally accepted ideas of his period and class. Even the most revolutionary thinker must speak – and think – in the language of his day.'[30]

The need for community (which as Cavell points out is the need for reason) does not only determine the limits of conceptual innovation, but also suggests two essential criteria by which such proposed innovations are to be judged: intelligibility and recognizable adequacy. On the one hand, proposed innovations may not be so far removed from the intuitive thought forms of the cultural community as to become *unintelligible* to its members in the sense that they do not 'know what to make of them'. On the other hand, proposed innovations must be *recognizably adequate* in the sense that other people are able to recognize them as more adequate to the 'strange demands life makes'. Innovations which fail to comply with these two criteria also fail to contribute to progress or improvement in the conceptual forms or ways of thinking of the community. It could happen of course that some innovative thinkers are 'ahead of their time' in the sense that the conceptual innovations they suggest are as yet either not intelligible or not recognizably adequate to their contemporaries. However, their innovations can only take effect as conceptual improvements to the way people think when succeeding generations come to 'know what to make of them' and recognize them as more adequate to the 'strange demands life makes'.

At this point a difficulty arises. Although these criteria are universally applicable in a formal sense, the way in which they are to be applied is not universally the same for all people. Thus intelligibility is a 'person-relative'[31] criterion in the sense that whether something is intelligible to someone depends on whether he or she is able to relate it to his or her own horizon of understanding. The same applies to recognizable adequacy to the demands of life. Not only are these demands not immutably the same for all people in all times, but whether someone recognizes the adequacy of a conceptual innovation also

---

[30] Nineham, *The Use and Abuse of the Bible*, 13–14.
[31] On 'person-relativity', see George I. Mavrodes, *Belief in God* (New York, 1970), ch. 2.

depends on his or her own horizon of understanding. Whether a proposed conceptual innovation is intelligible and recognizably adequate to more than one person thus depends in part on the extent to which they have a shared horizon of understanding. The community to whom specific conceptual forms and conceptual innovations are acceptable is limited and does not necessarily include everybody. Consequently D. Z. Phillips can say (with reference to Cavell and Wittgenstein) that

> when the word 'we' is used in such reminders as 'What we mean by...' a community of usage is invoked, but *not* necessarily a community to which *everyone* belongs... It follows that the reminders 'When we say...' and 'What we mean...' are not contradicted or falsified if an individual or group of individuals responds by saying, 'Well, *I* don't' or 'That's not true of us'. All that follows is that the responses show that those who make them are outside the community of usage which has been invoked.[32]

If the criteria for judging conceptual innovations are person-relative in this sense, what does this entail for the status of philosophical reflection as a scholarly discipline? Can an intellectual activity claim academic respectability if it cannot appeal to universally intersubjective criteria? There are various ways in which one could respond to this challenge. Two of the most fashionable contemporary responses are those of the relativist and descriptivist.

A relativist would agree that the acceptability of philosophical innovations is person-relative. What is intelligible to one person is not necessarily so for someone else with a different horizon of understanding, and philosophical innovations which are recognized as relevant within one cultural or historical setting are not necessarily recognized as such within another. However, the same is also true of art and literature. Many works of art and literature have a profound effect on the thinking of a period or culture because the ideas expressed in them are recognized by many as relevant to their deepest questions and to the fundamental issues of their time. Others, however, could fail

---

[32] Phillips, *Belief, Change and Forms of Life*, 17. See also Cavell, *The Claim of Reason*, 18–20.

to be affected in this way since they do not recognize these questions as their own nor the issues addressed as fundamental to their time or culture. This kind of relativity does not diminish the spiritual significance nor the intellectual respectability of art and literature. Similarly, it does not diminish the value of philosophical reflection.

The descriptivist agrees with this diagnosis but is not willing to leave it at that. More is required for philosophy than mere *intellectual* respectability. Philosophy must also earn *academic* standing by having its conclusions judged by universally accepted standards of scholarship. The relativist is satisfied to let the philosopher take on the role of a cultural prophet, the truth of whose utterances cannot be demonstrated by regular methods of scholarship, but depends on their being recognized as relevant by individuals within a specific cultural or historical setting. As a way out of this difficulty, the descriptivist suggests that the philosopher should describe the game of cultural prophecy rather than participating in it. The truth of the description can be demonstrated by regular methods of scholarship, even if the truth of the prophet's message cannot. On the basis of an extended analysis of recent German systematic theology, Anders Jeffner remarks on a similar 'flight to descriptivism' in many textbooks on dogmatics:

Instead of asserting a given theological doctrine, the theologian can simply describe it, adding that this is the doctrine of the Christian Church or of a specific Christian Church. To establish the truth of such a description, you need none of the special theological criteria of truth. The truth of the description can be demonstrated by the regular methods of scholarship, and to this extent the theologian is in the same boat as all scholars in the humanities. This, however, also means that he is no true doctrinal theologian. He is not trying to say anything about God, or about our relationship with God ... I cannot help but see the enormous amount of descriptions in the theological text-books as a flight from the problem of theological criteria of truth.[33]

[33] Anders Jeffner, *Theology and Integration* (Uppsala, 1987), 37–8. See also Jeffner, *Kriterien christlicher Glaubenslehre* (Göttingen, 1977). A similar tendency has also been noted by Dietrich Ritschl who remarks that during the last two decades Western theology 'in many places ... seems to dissolve into history (in the academic field) and sociology (in areas of practical concern)'. Ritschl, *The Logic of Theology* (London, 1986), 79.

Jeffner's conclusion applies to descriptivism in philosophy as well. The philosophical descriptivist avoids the problem of philosophical criteria by refusing to participate in the game of conceptual innovation.

Are the relativist and the descriptivist correct in their shared claim that the validity of conceptual innovations cannot be judged by generally accepted standards of scholarship? The trouble with this claim is that it assumes a sharp distinction between philosophical criteria that are person-relative and criteria that are not. In practice this distinction is misleading, for when judging the validity of proposed conceptual innovations we have to appeal to a variety of criteria, all of which are necessary but not one of which is sufficient. These criteria are not all person-relative, let alone person-relative to the same degree. The following criteria are all relevant in deciding the acceptability of proposed conceptual innovations. Of course, the fact that we can distinguish them in this way does not imply that they are logically independent of each other. On the contrary, they all presuppose each other in a variety of ways. We shall arrange them in an order of increasing person-relativity:

1 Is this innovation proposal internally *coherent*? And is it coherent with other conceptual forms which I am unable to set aside with integrity?
2 Is this innovation proposal *adequate* to the demands of life as I experience these in my cultural and historical situation?
3 Is this innovation *intelligible* to me, in the sense of being sufficiently consonant to the cultural tradition which constitutes my horizon of understanding for me to 'know what to make of it'?
4 Can I accept this innovation with *integrity*?

In varying degrees these criteria all involve both person-relative and intersubjective logical considerations. Thus internal coherence is not a purely logical criterion since individuals still have to see for themselves that something is internally coherent. Being able to accept an innovation proposal with integrity is not purely person-relative, since this depends very much on the logical coherence with other conceptual forms which a person accepts (criterion 1). Although adequacy of the demands of life is relative to the historical and cultural situation in which one finds oneself, it is always possible to argue for or against the relevance or adequacy of a proposed innovation, and the validity of such arguments can again be judged by intersubjective logical means.

The role of person-relative considerations becomes relatively greater as the conceptual forms in question are more subject to cultural variation and historical change. Thus such considerations will carry relatively more weight in deciding the acceptability of moral judgements and religious beliefs than in deciding the validity of logical operations which are relatively free from cultural variation. The significance of this difference should not however be overestimated, since it remains a difference of degree and not of kind, and since all the above criteria remain relevant to the evaluation of *all* conceptual forms, including religious beliefs, moral judgements, knowledge claims in science, and pure logical operations. Nowhere can the intersubjective criteria be ignored: logical considerations apply to all our thinking in all contexts, because if we do not honour them, we will contradict ourselves and deny whatever we are trying to assert. In this way we will fail to assert anything at all! Nor, on the other hand, can person-relative considerations ever be eliminated. Even something as intersubjective as a valid deductive argument succeeds in proving its conclusion only to those who can accept the truth of its premises with integrity.[34] However forceful an argument may be, it never forces. For this reason Augustine was right in pointing out that however much a pupil can learn from his teacher, there is one thing he must always discover for himself, that is, that what his teacher tells him is true, 'because no one can discern the truth for him in his stead'.[35]

[34] See Antony Flew, *An Introduction to Western Philosophy* (London, 1971), 23–4, and Mavrodes, *Belief in God*, ch. 2.

[35] Augustine, *De Magistro*, 12.40, in *Augustine: Earlier Writings* (Philadelphia, PA, 1953), 96–7. See also Etienne Gilson, *The Christian Philosophy of Saint Augustine* (London, 1961), 70.

In striving after rationality, scientific inquiry and critical scholarship appeal to intersubjective criteria since these provide a basis for consensus. As Stanley Cavell says, 'the wish and search for community are the wish and search for reason'.[36] However, since person-relative considerations can never be completely eliminated, the intersubjective criteria, although necessary, can never be sufficient to force conclusions.

Every sound argument 'forces', in the sense that it limits the available options even though no argument can ever be 'completely compulsive', if by that were to be meant – what never is meant – that it blocks up literally every alternative to accepting its conclusion. For ... any valid deductive argument can as such be either a proof of its conclusions or a disproof of one of its premises.[37]

Although person-relative considerations always play a part in deciding the acceptability of proposed conceptual innovations, this clearly does not exclude the possibility of evaluating them in a scholarly way with an appeal to intersubjective logical criteria. Even if such scholarly inquiry does not force conclusions, it nevertheless limits the options between which a choice could be made in the light of more person-relative considerations. As we suggested in section 1.3 above, philosophers reflect on *possible* conceptual forms, in order to see whether they are coherent and relevant, and in order to see what the implications would be if we were to accept them as our own. In this way the aim of scholarly inquiry in philosophy is not necessarily to force conclusions but rather to limit and clarify our conceptual options, and thus to contribute to progress in our thinking.

1.5 PHILOSOPHICAL THEOLOGY

Philosophical reflection aims at clarifying and limiting our conceptual options.[38] The extent of the limitation depends on the range of criteria involved. The more person-relative criteria are involved in the reflection, the greater the limits placed on

---

[36] Cavell, *The Claim of Reason*, 20.
[37] Flew, *An Introduction to Western Philosophy*, 24.
[38] For an illuminating comparison of this view on philosophical reflection with other views, see David A. Pailin, *Groundwork of Philosophy of Religion*, 2nd edn (London, 1989), 21–32.

our conceptual options. This point can be illustrated by comparing various levels of reflection regarding the conceptual forms of religious or ideological views of life. The most general level of reflection here is that of *philosophical theology* which tries to determine which conceptual forms can be accepted without contradiction. The next level is that of *confessional theology* (church dogmatics) which goes a step further by involving confessional criteria and trying to determine which conceptual forms can be accepted without becoming untrue to the community of faith (or the religious tradition, or the ideological group, and so on). A final level of reflection is that of *personal faith* in which each person must determine for him- or herself which conceptual forms he or she can accept without losing his or her integrity.

As the range of criteria appealed to is increased in these three levels of reflection, the range of conceptual options left open is progressively limited and the size of the community of thought appealed to is progressively narrowed down. To the extent that philosophical theology limits itself to applying general logical criteria, it seeks to achieve a consensus including everybody. The group for which it aims to speak includes all people. As we pointed out in section 1.3 above, there is of course no guarantee that such broad consensus will be achieved. 'For all Wittgenstein's claims about what we say, he is always at the same time aware that others might not agree, that a given person or group (a "tribe") might *not* share our criteria.'[39] However, as Cavell shows, if I were not to share Wittgenstein's claim about 'what we say', he would not thereby be obliged to amend his claim in order to account for my difference. 'He hasn't said something false about "us"; he has learned that there is no us (yet, maybe never) to say anything about. What is wrong with his statement is that he made it to the wrong party.'[40]

Confessional dogmatics does not aim at a consensus including all people. It claims to speak only for the community of faith. For this reason it appeals not only to general logical criteria but also to those criteria which are definitive for the thought of the

---

[39] Cavell, *The Claim of Reason*, 18. [40] Ibid., 19–20.

community of faith. This includes not only the hermeneutical dialogue with what David Tracy calls the 'classic texts'[41] of the community of faith (e.g. the Bible or the Koran or the Communist Manifesto, etc.), but also an attempt to remain faithful to those doctrines which, as George Lindbeck argues, function as 'communally authoritative teachings regarding beliefs and practices that are considered essential to the identity or welfare of the group in question. They may be formally stated or informally operative, but in any case they indicate what constitutes faithful adherence to a community.'[42] Of course such criteria are not immutable. Like human thought in general, the thought of a community of faith is subject to historical and cultural change. Thus changes may take place in the way a confessional community interprets its classic texts and in the doctrines which are operative and recognized as authoritative within that community. For this reason confessional dogmatics, like philosophy, has an innovative role to fulfil with respect to the thought of the community. In fulfilling this role, however, it remains faithful to a specific community of faith to the extent that it seeks conceptual innovations which are intelligible and recognizably adequate within that community.

In a sense personal faith also tries to find a kind of consensus, that is, the consensus that each believer must have with him- or herself in order to believe with integrity and not remain 'in two minds' about his or her faith. At this level all faith is truly personal. In the words of Wilfred Cantwell Smith: 'My faith is an act that *I* make, myself, naked before God.'[43] Of course this does not exclude the possibility that others might share my personal faith by recognizing it as similar to their own. In fact all believers desire that their own personal faith might correspond to that of the community of faith, for only in that case will they be able to identify with the community without sacrificing their own personal integrity in order to do so.

In closing we can now draw four important conclusions regarding the nature of philosophical theology. First of all,

---

[41] David Tracy, *The Analogical Imagination* (London, 1981), ch. 3.
[42] George A. Lindbeck, *The Nature of Doctrine* (Philadelphia, PA, 1984), 74.
[43] Wilfred Cantwell Smith, *The Meaning and End of Religion* (London, 1978), 191.

philosophical theology in the sense defined in this chapter is clearly distinct from all 'natural theology' in which an attempt is made to provide 'a conceptual grounding for the faith such that its rationality and the irrationality of its denial can be demonstrated'.[44] We have argued that philosophical theology does not demonstrate what must be believed. It merely tries to limit the conceptual options to those that can be accepted without contradiction. In the end the decision as to which of the coherent options we are to choose has to be taken on other grounds (religious, ideological, personal, etc.) than those appealed to by philosophy. Faith cannot be derived from (or 'based on') philosophy.

Secondly, to the extent that the philosophical theologian limits him- or herself to applying general logical criteria rather than the criteria of a specific confessional community, the practice of philosophical theology does not presuppose allegiance to any specific view of life or confessional position. On this level of reflection everybody can participate together irrespective of their confessional or ideological allegiance: the theist and the atheist, the Christian and the humanist, the Buddhist and the communist, and so on. Although philosophical theology reflects on the faith, it is not derived from (or 'based on') any specific faith.

Thirdly, to the extent that the philosophical theologian seeks a consensus among all people and not only among the adherents of a specific view of life (religion, ideology, etc.), he is free to analyse the conceptual forms of every or any view of life. All people try to make sense of their lives and their experience of the world by means of the conceptual resources of a view of life, even though all do not appeal to the same view of life. Hence the reflection practised by the philosophical theologian includes an inquiry both into the nature of views of life in general (what sort of conceptual resources are needed to make sense of life?) and into the conceptual grammar of specific views of life (what would be the implications of making sense of life by means of the conceptual resources of specific views of life?).

---

[44] Phillips, *Belief, Change and Forms of Life*, 116.

Finally, philosophical theology does not presuppose any confessional allegiance; nor does it provide a rational foundation or justification for any confessional position. From this it does not follow, however, that philosophical theology and confessional dogmatics have nothing to do with each other. On the contrary, it would be very difficult in practice to limit oneself to one of these and to avoid the other altogether. On the one hand, confessional dogmatics is not different from but more than philosophical theology. It is not satisfied with finding out which conceptual possibilities are coherent, but wants to go further and find out which of the coherent possibilities are intelligible and recognizably adequate within the horizon of understanding of the community of faith. On the other hand, the philosophical theologian is not only a philosopher, but also a human being who tries to make sense of life and the world by means of the conceptual resources of the cultural, ideological or religious tradition with which he or she can identify with integrity. Hence, in the final analysis the philosophical theologian cannot be satisfied with reflecting on abstract conceptual possibilities, but must seek to understand those possibilities which he or she can make his or her own with integrity. When this happens, philosophical theology turns into the Anselmian enterprise of *fides quaerens intellectum*: faith seeking understanding.[45]

This view on philosophical theology is well summarized in the words of Charles M. Wood concerning philosophical reflection on the Christian faith:

That effort, and that sort of involvement of philosophy in the theological task, is a far cry from any attempt to provide a philosophical foundation of Christianity. It does not ask philosophy to

[45] 'In the last few years, many influential philosophers of religion have once again turned their attention to specific theological doctrines. Typically, these philosophers are not trying to prove or establish these doctrines philosophically. Rather, in the spirit of Anselm, they assume a particular doctrine as a given topic of religious concern and set about to analyze its meaning and assess whether it can be affirmed by a rational person.' M. L. Peterson, 'Philosophy and theological doctrine: Can philosophy illuminate religious belief?', in Peterson et al., *Reason and Religious Belief: An Introduction to the Philosophy of Religion* (Oxford and New York, 1991), 254. For an example of this approach, see Thomas V. Morris, *Anselmian Explorations* (Notre Dame, IN, 1987).

swear allegiance to the Christian commonwealth, nor to provide a home for wandering Christians in search of more security than their faith can give them. Philosophy may neither bestow nor ground the sense of Christian witness; but as an instrument to aid in displaying that sense so that it is accessible for reflection, judgement, and participation, it has a vital role in the ongoing theological venture of faith seeking understanding.[46]

[46] Charles M. Wood, 'Theology and philosophy: response to D. Z. Phillips', *Perkins Journal*, 32 (1979), 19.

CHAPTER 2

Can we speak about God?

2.1 THE LIMITS OF GOD-TALK

In the previous chapter we argued that logical coherence is one of the necessary conditions which every acceptable proposal for conceptualizing the faith should fulfil. For this reason philosophical reflection has a necessary role to play within systematic theology. To some extent all systematic theology is therefore a philosophical enterprise. This claim is often rejected by theologians, on the grounds that the faith which they proclaim transcends the limits of logical coherence. Since the logical criteria of philosophy do not apply here, philosophical reflection is irrelevant to theology and 'philosophical theology' is a contradiction in terms. If, as in this book, we want to defend the necessary role of philosophical theology within the enterprise of theology as such, we will have to take these doubts seriously and provide an answer to them. In this chapter we will try to show in some detail that, although this view on the nature of theology has some point, it is in the end self-defeating and therefore invalid.

In section 1.2 above we argued that, following Wittgenstein, we can consider concepts as fundamental forms of thought, or mental capacities (as Peter Geach calls them)[1] which we employ in our interaction with each other in the world. As such, they also form the basic elements in our speech. Our concepts are expressed in our words. Since thought, speech and action in fact form a well-knit unity in human life, our concepts are expressed

[1] Peter Geach, *Mental Acts* (London, 1957), ch. 5.

33

not only in what we say, but in all our actions in the various areas of human life. As Wittgenstein puts it: 'To imagine a language means to imagine a form of life.'[2]

Given that life is indivisible, our thought also constitutes a unity and the various thought forms or concepts are all related to each other in the unity of life. Religious concepts are no exception and have no special conceptual status. They are ordinary concepts, which are used in a specific area of life, namely the area of faith. Alasdair MacIntyre observes that expressions such as 'the language of the Bible' and 'religious language' should not obscure the fact that the language is neither more nor less than ordinary Hebrew or English, albeit being used for a special purpose. He quotes Sir Edwyn Hoskins in this connection, who wrote: 'The language of the Holy Spirit is New Testament Greek.'[3] When we relate to God through words and actions in the liturgy, or when we think or talk about God and our relationship with him in doing theology or in preaching, we are using the same concepts that we use in our thinking about each other and in our relationship with each other. We speak about God and with God in personal terms.

Just as with concepts in other areas of life, religious concepts often present us with *conceptual problems* on account of the fact that they behave paradoxically and apparently contradict each other. While believers say that God is eternal and unchangeable, they also maintain that God became incarnate and was subject to change. Believers speak of God as a Father, who is eternal, or as a Son, who performed actions in history, or as a Spirit, who is present everywhere, yet they maintain that this does not involve three different gods, but just one. On the one hand, believers hold that if people do not turn to God, they will remain eternally guilty, on the other they assert that people cannot achieve this conversion by themselves, because only God can bring about the conversion within them. On the one hand, believers claim that God is almighty and perfectly good, and on

[2] Ludwig Wittgenstein, *Philosophical Investigations* (Oxford, 1953), i, 19. For a more extended treatment of the theory assumed here about the nature of concepts and their relationship to words and reality, see my *Theology and Philosophical Inquiry* (London, 1981), ch. 3. See also note 19 below.

[3] Alasdair MacIntyre (ed.), *Metaphysical Beliefs* (London, 1957), 176.

the other they admit that God allows a great deal of affliction in the world, even though he could have prevented it. On the one hand, believers say that God listens to the prayers of their children, on the other they hold that God is unchangeable and so is not to be turned away from what has been decided in his eternal intention.

How should we regard these paradoxes? Are they in principle resolvable conceptual problems like paradoxes in other areas of life? Does the resolution of religious paradoxes form part of the agenda for systematic theology? If so, philosophical reflection has an essential role to play in systematic theology. Or are they symptomatic of the fact that we have here reached the limits of meaningful language, and hence of the domain where philosophical inquiry is valid? This last question is given an affirmative answer from two quite different quarters. There is remarkable agreement on this point between the position to which many theologians adhere and the stand taken by certain critics of religion.

It is important that we distinguish between three forms which the criticism of religion can take: *psychological* criticism of religion (where religious belief is rejected as being a form of psychic projection), *epistemological* criticism of religion (where the knowledge claims of religion are rejected as without any epistemological basis), and *logical* criticism of religion (where religious belief is rejected as being logically incoherent). In this last form of criticism, the paradoxes of the belief are interpreted as contradictions which are necessarily untrue. Through such paradoxical statements things are affirmed and at the same time are by implication denied, so that in the final analysis, nothing is said at all. It is impossible therefore for paradoxes to be believed: we cannot believe that circles are square, or that an unchangeable being is subject to change! According to these critics, such paradoxes merely show that religious beliefs are a bunch of contradictions. Each paradox is simply another argument for the rejection of religion. God-talk or theo-logy is impossible because it is logically incoherent.[4]

---

[4] See for example Bernard Williams, 'Tertullian's Paradox', in A. Flew and A. MacIntyre (eds.), *New Essays in Philosophical Theology* (London, 1955). For a

Some theologians are in agreement with these critics to the extent that they also hold that belief is *in its very nature* paradoxical. We can only speak of God in paradoxes. Paradoxes are in fact a necessary consequence of religion being concerned with the *unutterable*. The reality of God transcends our human logic and our human concepts. Thus it is not surprising that when we want to speak about a transcendent Being such as God, our concepts will appear paradoxical.

Apart from its relevance for the aim of this book, there are three reasons why we should examine this last standpoint carefully. First because it is a position which is implicitly or explicitly held by many theologians. Secondly, there are important elements of truth in this position: God *is* in a certain sense beyond understanding, dwelling 'in inaccessible light'. In the third place, without further qualification this viewpoint would in fact entail the end of both theology and the proclamation of the faith. Thus it is of great importance for us to gain some clarity concerning the limits of God-talk or theology.

There are three kinds of limits which should be distinguished here. Firstly, there are *religious* limits to what we can say about God. God is the Holy One about whom we may only speak with reticence and awe. Secondly, there are *epistemological* limits. Our knowledge of God is limited and accordingly there is also a limit to what we are justifiably able to say about God. Thirdly, there are *semantic* limits, because words undergo shifts in meaning when we use them in the context of faith. God is not like other people and even if we use the same words in talking about both, this does not mean that the words have precisely the same meaning in the two cases.[5]

What is it that determines the semantic limits of God-talk? Some people hold that these limits are determined by an *infinite*

---

demonstration of the claim that nothing can be said by means of contradictions, see *inter alia* K. R. Popper, *Conjectures and Refutations* (London, 1963), ch. 15.

[5] As we shall see, this does not mean that the meanings are quite different either! See in this connection William P. Alston's plea for 'univocal predication', for example in his paper on 'Functionalism and theological language' in T. V. Morris (ed.), *The Concept of God* (Oxford, 1987), 21–40. See also the first part of Alston's *Divine Nature and Human Language* (Ithaca, NY, 1989).

qualitative difference between God and human persons; again, others propose that the semantic limits are here determined by the *analogy* between God and human persons; yet others relate these limits to the *metaphorical language* and the *conceptual models* that we use in our talk about God. Let us look further into these possibilities.

2.2 THE INFINITE QUALITATIVE DIFFERENCE

1 Paradox and dialectic

A view which is often defended in theology is that belief in paradoxes is not only *possible* (people do in fact believe in paradoxes), but also *necessary* since the reality of God transcends our human logic and our human concepts. Everything that we say about God with human concepts is incorrect (because these concepts are not applicable to God) and should therefore be qualified by affirming the contrary. This is the source of the paradoxical nature of our talk about God. Thus for example W. H. Austin argues that 'the affirmation–negation paradox is of fundamental importance in theology, giving expression to the principle that the religious ultimate is beyond all human concepts, so that what is affirmed of it must also be denied'.[6]

The Dutch dialectical theologian G. C. Van Niftrik also defends this view.[7] He argues that if we are going to talk about God in human words and concepts, we must be aware of the fact that each human word and concept falls short of what we actually need to say and cannot put into words, namely the reality of God. Each human word and concept is inadequate, as such, for *this* reality, the reality of God. One word is not enough to say what there is to say; each word must be followed directly by another word, because the reality cannot be encompassed in one word. The mysterious truth of that God, who is the Wholly Other, and dwells in the inaccessible light, cannot be expressed by means of a direct word. If we have asserted something, then

---

[6] William H. Austin, *Waves, Particles and Paradoxes* (Houston, TX, 1967), 49. See also chapter 2 of Ninian Smart, *The Philosophy of Religion* (New York, 1970) for a helpful analysis of this kind of position.

[7] G. C. Van Niftrik, *Een Beroerder Israëls* (Nijkerk, 1949), 54.

we must – since it is about God – immediately interrupt ourselves, and qualify our Yes by a No and our No by a Yes. In
short, paradoxes in belief are not necessarily untrue assertions,
as the critics of religion maintain, but a necessary consequence
of the fact that God is *indescribable* since he transcends the
domain in which human concepts are applicable.

Three remarks can be made with respect to this viewpoint.
Firstly, we must grant the critics of religion that it is impossible
to believe contradictions. A contradictory statement always
asserts something, and then retracts what has been asserted,
with the result that in the end nothing is left to be believed. This
does not deny that people often do believe things without taking
into consideration that there is a logical inconsistency. They are
not aware of all the implications of the propositions that they
accept and so are also not aware of the possible contradictions
involved in their beliefs. Should the contradictions be made
plain, however, they are obliged to change their beliefs, in order
to make them consistent. For we cannot accept an explicit
contradiction and maintain that we have still made a meaningful statement.

Secondly, in what sense do we say of God that he is
'indescribable' in human concepts? An analogy is often
proposed here with the indescribability of certain experiences or
feelings. Indeed the intensity of certain experiences or feelings
cannot always be evoked in another person by words alone. But
this does not amount to saying that the feelings cannot be
indicated by words (as feelings or experiences of gratitude, pain,
joy, etc.) and in this way to be distinguished from other feelings.
Feelings are not in this sense beyond the range of human
concepts. In what sense, then, is God?

Thirdly, if *none* of our concepts are applicable to God, how
can we indicate who it is that we consider to be indescribable?
Do we not in that case use a concept ('God') to refer to
something which, according to this view, by definition cannot
be referred to by means of a concept?

2 *Referential language*

One proposal for dealing with the problem is the following. On the one hand, we can maintain on the basis of the theory of the infinite qualitative difference that God cannot be *described*, but still admit that it is possible to *refer* to him. Religious language is then referential by nature rather than descriptive. The word 'God' is a name, by which we refer to a being, but it is not a descriptive term. Religious symbols and propositions are so many signs that point in the direction of that place where we can experience God, but are not descriptions of him.

This position is defended for example by the Dutch theologian R. J. Mooi in the following way:[8] The nature of God is in principle beyond any image that we can form about him. God is to such a degree the Wholly Other that he is in principle unimaginable. The difficulty of religious language is that it necessarily remains human language and for that very reason cannot be transcended. If, on the other hand, this language could be transcended, it would then become 'un-speakable' for us. The question is inevitably: Is a religious language conceivable which on the one hand has transcended human speech, but on the other hand is still 'speakable'? According to Mooi there must be a positive answer to this question. This involves religious language of a *referential* character. Thus Mooi holds that there is no religious language other than language of a referential character. There are also no other religious ideas than those of a referential nature. It is precisely in the reference that the religious content of the language, thought or idea lies. The reference coincides with a leap, far from the human manner of thought, but not cut off from rationality, a leap which goes forth into transcendence. That which is referred to has no direct relationship with the referential language as such. The linguistic content, the object of reference, is not the content of the referential language, but the transcended content of it. By means of the reference a fumbling acknowledgement has become possible, a 'conjecture', which, as it were, constitutes

[8] R. J. Mooi, 'Het verwijzend karakter van het godsdienstig spreken', *In de Waagschaal*, 9 (1980–1), 127–9.

the essence of religious language and thought. Thus the Bible needs to be understood in the first place as a collection of writings where there is referential talk about the actions of God.

The difficulty with this position is that the opposition between reference and description cannot be maintained. Reference is indeed the identification of that to which reference is made, distinguishing it from everything else. This assumes that it is in principle describable as 'identifiable in this way'. Thus the use of names to distinguish persons or things *assumes* a procedure to identify what is being pointed out, and therefore its description as 'an entity that can be identified by this procedure'. In the Bible, God is often identified by being related to concrete situations and people: the One who led Israel out of Egypt, sent his Son into the world, and so on. This also implies a description. Moreover, if it is possible to have a conscious relationship with God or to experience the presence of God, then he must also be describable in this respect as the one who is experienced in this or that way.

In short, if we can refer to God, or relate God to the world of our experience, or experience God's presence, then he cannot be beyond the range of all human concepts. At least some descriptive terms must be applicable to him.

3 The language of revelation

If our human concepts should be in part applicable to God and in part not, where does the boundary lie? Perhaps this question can be answered as follows: We experience God only as he has revealed himself to us and not as he actually is in himself. Our concepts are therefore applicable to God's revelation, but not to him as he is in himself. Every attempt to speak about *that* is therefore paradoxical, because in himself God transcends the domain where human concepts are applicable. God reveals himself to us in terms of aspects of our world that are experienced by us. In himself God is indeed the Wholly Other, who in no way fits into the world of our experience. Thus there is still what Van Niftrik, following Kierkegaard, calls 'an infinite qualitative difference between eternity and time, between God and man'.

What should we understand by 'an infinite qualitative difference'? It is important here to distinguish between: 1. non-identity (for example, between two plates in the same dinner service); 2. a quantitative difference (for example, between two plates and four plates in the same dinner service); and 3. a qualitative difference (for example, between a plate and a platter). When two entities differ from each other *qualitatively*, this implies that some properties which can truthfully be attributed to the one cannot truthfully be attributed to the other. If the qualitative difference is *infinite*, this will presumably mean that no properties which can truthfully be attributed to the one can truthfully be attributed to the other. An infinite qualitative difference between God and the world of our experience would imply that no concepts which are applicable to the world of our experience can be truthfully applied to God – not even the concept 'holy'.

This proposal has unacceptable consequences. Firstly, given that God reveals himself to us in this world (and in terms of this world), the theory of an infinite qualitative difference implies that no concept that we use to describe a *revelation* of God is applicable to God himself. Thus there would exist no correspondence at all between God himself and his revelation, with the consequence that it would be nonsensical to continue to speak of a *revelation*.

Secondly, when we do speak about God, we use the same words that we use to speak about the people and things which we encounter in this world. Our descriptive words derive their meaning from the way we use them in describing our finite experience. The theory of the infinite qualitative difference therefore implies that all words which we use to speak about God are uprooted from the meaning they have for us. There is, for example, no similarity in meaning at all between the word 'love' with reference to God and the word 'love' with reference to people. It is no help to use another word in order to avoid such complete equivocation, given the fact that the same difficulty arises with respect to *all* other words. The result of this is agnosticism with respect to God.

The theory of the infinite qualitative difference between God and his revelation in this world is thus untenable, since on the one hand it contradicts the doctrine of the revelation of God and on the other leads to an agnosticism.

4 Limited but adequate theo-logy

By revealing himself to us, God breaks through the *epistemological* and thereby also the *semantic* barrier between him and us. There is no gulf between God and his revelation. If we assume that there is a gulf, we make the concept 'revelation' vacuous. To the extent that we know God's revelation, we know God *himself*. In this way the epistemological barrier is broken down and God becomes knowable for us. When we speak about God's revelation, we are speaking about God himself. In this way the semantic barrier is also broken down and it becomes possible for us to speak about God.

The extent of God's revelation determines the *epistemological* and along with it the *semantic* limits to God-talk. The fact that God's revelation enables us to know him and to speak about him does not entail that God cannot be more than what he has revealed to us about himself, nor that our assertions about him could provide more than a very incomplete description of him. On the contrary, we know God only to the extent that he reveals himself to us; and we cannot say more about God than we know about him. In this sense God's revelation determines the limits of what we know and can say about him.[9]

Furthermore, even though our knowledge of God is limited and our descriptions of him incomplete, they are certainly adequate for our needs as believers. Through his revelation, God makes it possible for us to know as much about him and to say as much about him as is necessary for us in order to be able to live as persons in relation to him. Our knowledge about God and the possibility of being able to speak about God are therefore adequate for a life *coram Deo*.

[9] The differences and the similarities between different forms of revelation (especially revelation in history, the Bible, nature, religious experience, etc.) is a separate issue which we will not discuss here. We are concerned here with the claim that we can know God only to the extent that God has made himself known to us – irrespective of the means by which or the way in which this is done.

Similar limits exist for *all knowledge* and *all descriptions* and not only for our knowledge of and talk about God.[10] If, for example, I had to describe a road accident, I could say: 'There were a number of casualties.' That would be true but very incomplete. I could go on making my description more complete until I reach the epistemological limits and no longer *know* anything to say. After that I could extend the epistemological limits by finding out more. Eventually an end would be reached. At a certain moment I will terminate my description, when it is *adequate*. At which precise point my description is adequate depends on the purpose of the description, my skill as a narrator and the ability of my listener to understand.

In short: on the basis of God's revelation it is possible to know him in a limited but adequate manner, and thus also to speak about him. This implies that there can be no infinite qualitative difference between God and us. Indeed, if there were an infinite qualitative difference, then none of our concepts would be applicable to God, no knowledge about him would be possible, and we would end up in agnosticism. This does not detract from the fact that God is different from other people. At most we could speak of an *analogy* between God and human persons, that is, a partial similarity and a partial difference. What is the nature and extent of this analogy and how do we find out about it?

2.3 ANALOGY

1 Attribution and proportion

The question about the semantic limits of talk about God seems to present us with a dilemma. If, on the one hand, the words that we use to speak about God (for example, wisdom, power, authority, king, shepherd, etc.) have the same meaning as when we use them to talk about people, this implies that God shares certain characteristics with his creatures. This would entail an anthropomorphism which fails to do justice to God's trans-

---

[10] Cf. Smart, *The Philosophy of Religion*, 69–70.

cendence. We also fail to avoid this kind of anthropomorphism by merely accepting a (possibly infinite) *quantitative* difference between God and his creatures. In this connection, R. J. Mooi argues that we do not say anything meaningful about God when we attempt to extend our own theological statements in the direction of eternity: for example, by changing the statement 'God is good' into 'God is infinitely good', or by saying in place of 'God shows mercy' that 'God shows the perfection of mercy', or by changing 'God is love' into 'God is the pure, highest love'. Such extensions of our religious language with qualifications of infinity and eternity do not bring us any further. In fact, our images remain exactly what they are and they do not change essentially through the addition of an infinity marker. Our notions remain nothing more than *our* human notions and they fail to be qualitatively transcended.[11]

When, on the other hand, the words that we use to speak about God have a completely different meaning from when we use them to speak about human beings, we revert to the claim of the infinite qualitative difference. As we have already shown, this leads to agnosticism: we no longer know what our words mean when we speak about God.

A solution to this dilemma is usually sought in terms of *analogy*. The characteristics of God are not identical with those of human beings, but they are analogous (partly similar) to those of human beings. The question now is whether it is possible to speak about God in this way and still to maintain a qualitative difference between God and his creatures. In other words, is it possible to find a form of analogy which does not assume any identity of the properties between the analogous entities? Can we have our cake and eat it? To this purpose attempts have been made to use the analogy of *attribution* and the analogy of *proportionality*.[12]

The analogy of attribution links two analogous entities which are different in many respects. One of these entities possesses the characteristic attributed to both in the 'proper' or ordinary

[11] Mooi, 'Het verwijzend karakter', 127.
[12] See F. Ferre, *Language, Logic and God* (London, 1962), ch. 6.

sense, while the other possesses this characteristic in a derived sense. Thus we can for example call someone 'healthy'. Besides using the word 'healthy' for people, we can also use it in a sentence such as 'The air in the mountains is healthy'. In both cases the word 'healthy' is used, but it is clear that the person about whom we are speaking is not healthy in the same way as the air in the mountains. The air is 'healthy' in a derived sense of the word, because it makes the people who breathe it healthy in the ordinary sense of the word. In the analogy of attribution one analogical characteristic comes forth from the other: the one is an effect, the other is a cause. Applied to theology, where God and human persons are the entities in question, we have the following situation: in the statements 'God is wise' and 'Socrates is wise' the meaning of the word 'wise' has the ordinary meaning in the second statement; when we say that God is wise, we are able to do that given the fact that he is the source, the cause or fountain of 'wisdom'. If we wish to be precise, when we use the analogy of attribution, we are also saying 'Socrates is wise' *and* 'God is the cause or origin of all wisdom'. God is thus wise in an 'original' sense, because he is the origin of all the wisdom (in the ordinary sense of the word) which we encounter in human persons.

In the analogy of proportionality, the attribute which is ascribed in two different statements is the same, but must be seen in relation to the nature of the different entities to which it is ascribed. For example, in the two expressions 'the red shop steward' and 'the red shop door', the word 'red' is used *equivocally* (with more than one meaning). Here there is no question of a common characteristic. If however we call two identically painted letter boxes 'red', then the word is used unequivocally: we ascribe *the same* characteristic to two entities. We can also call both Jack's hair and the sunset red, and in this case both things have the common property 'red', but in a way appropriate to their distinct natures. Indeed, the sunset is red in a way characteristic for sunsets, and Jack's hair is red in quite a different way, namely the way in which people's hair can be red. In this case we are using the analogy of proportionality. This form of analogy, applied to our language about God, results in the following. Consider again the two sentences 'God is wise' and 'Socrates is wise'. In terms of the analogy of proportionality, these mean respectively that God is wise in the way in which God can be wise, and Socrates is wise in the way in which human beings can be wise. God's wisdom relates to God's nature, just as human wisdom relates to human nature. Or put differently, the relationship of God's wisdom to his nature is the same as the relationship of human wisdom to human nature. In the analogy of proportionality the analogous entities both possess the relevant characteristic, but each possesses it in relation (or proportion) to its own nature. The way in which an entity possesses the relevant characteristic is determined by its own nature. God's wisdom is in no way identical with that of Socrates, because God's nature is quite different from that of a human being.

Both these forms of analogy entail serious difficulties. The analogy of proportionality states that human beings are wise in their own way (in accordance with their own nature) and that God is wise in a completely different (divine) way, in accordance with his nature. But that does not get us any further, given that we now have a comparison involving too many unknowns: human wisdom stands in relation to human nature as divine wisdom stands in relation to divine nature. But we do not know the nature of God in himself, and we want to define his manner of being wise precisely in terms of his nature. God's nature is not accessible to us, nor therefore is the way in which he is wise. It follows that in using the analogy of proportionality we are saying no more than that God is not wise in the same way as a human person is wise. But then we are still unable to say positively in what sense God is in fact wise. This is equally true for all the other concepts that we wish to apply to God. The analogy of proportionality thus takes us no further than a negative theology.

Objections can also be made against the analogy of attribution. This form of analogy does not say anything about the characteristics which God in fact possesses, but only tells us of which characteristics he is the source: 'Jack is healthy' but 'the air is health-giving', 'Socrates is wise' but 'God is the source of wisdom'. Furthermore, with the analogy of attribution there is no end to the list of God's characteristics. As creator and cause of everything, he is the source of all the characteristics of his creatures. The analogy of attribution seems to leave us free to call God 'warm', 'multi-coloured' and 'heavy', because he is the source of all warm, multi-coloured and heavy objects! We could add the limitation: not all terms are to be applied to God in this way; only the terms which apply to his nature. But then we would have to know God's nature, and we have already said that we do not know God's nature.

We are therefore still faced with the problem: How can we say something meaningful about God without assuming that God shares certain characteristics with his creatures? Neither the analogy of attribution nor the analogy of proportionality can give us a satisfactory answer here.

2 *Analogy and agnosticism*

The position of I. M. Crombie[13] is a remarkable half-way attempt to cut through this knot. Crombie grants that God in himself is unknown to us. Hence we speak about him in images and not in literal assertions. Given that these images have been made available to us in God's revelation, we accept on his authority that they are applicable to him. However, we have no means of establishing *how* they apply to him. In short, there is a real analogy (common characteristics) between God and us and this analogy forms the basis of our talk about God. Consequently our words are not devoid of meaning when we talk about God. However, we do not know what the content of this analogy is. Crombie in effect rejects the theory of the infinite qualitative difference and proposes that there actually are common characteristics between God and human creatures. But he still ends with agnosticism, since according to him, we do not know which these common characteristics are. If we wish to resolve these problems, then we have to go further than Crombie and indicate a way in which it is possible to establish what the

[13] In Flew and MacIntyre (eds.), *New Essays in Philosophical Theology*, 118–24.

common characteristics are that form a basis for our talk about God. Thomas Aquinas and Karl Barth both try to provide an answer, each in his own way.

3 'Analogia entis'

In his theory of the *analogia entis*, Aquinas tries to solve these problems.[14] As we have said, the analogy of attribution only allows us to say which characteristics God is the source of, but not which characteristics he *has*. This means, on the one hand, that the analogy of attribution provides us with no common characteristics which could be the basis for our talk about God, and on the other hand, that no knowledge of God's characteristics is possible, so that we cannot avoid agnosticism with respect to God. Aquinas tries to interpret the analogy of attribution in such a way that these objections can be overcome.

To this end, Aquinas links the analogy of attribution with two assumptions. Firstly, he assumes that effects are by definition analogous to their causes. On this assumption, creatures necessarily have shared characteristics with their Creator. Secondly, Aquinas links the analogy of attribution with the analogy of proportionality: the Creator has these characteristics in a way that befits his own nature and not in the way that befits the nature of creatures. As source of all wisdom, God is wise in a *divine* way, that is, *perfectly* wise in contrast to his creatures, who reflect his wisdom in very imperfect ways.

With respect to how we can know God's characteristics, Aquinas holds that the theory of analogy can itself be the basis for a natural theology by means of which we can come to know at least in part which characteristics God has in common with his creatures. By means of the cosmological argument, we can *demonstrate* that God is the First Cause of everything. Since

---

[14] See Thomas Aquinas, *Summa Theologiae*, 1.13, especially arts. 2, 3, 5 and 6. For a contemporary presentation of Aquinas' doctrine of analogy, defending especially the analogy of proper proportionality against recent criticisms by Frederick Ferré and others, see James F. Ross, 'Analogy as a rule of meaning for religious language', *International Philosophical Quarterly*, 30 (1961), 468–502. See also his *Philosophical Theology*, 2nd edn (Indianapolis, 1980), 51–63, and in general his *Portraying Analogy* (Cambridge, 1982).

effects necessarily reflect the characteristics of their causes, it follows that we can derive some knowledge of the characteristics of the First Cause from our knowledge of its effects in the created world.

In following this strategy, Aquinas departs from the claim that there is an absolute qualitative difference between God and human creatures and proposes that God has certain characteristics in common with his creatures. He would also reject an agnosticism like that proposed by Crombie: we know by means of natural theology which characteristics are shared and thus are the basis for our talk about God. Furthermore, the *analogia entis* is itself the basis for this natural theology: God can be known from the characteristics (*ex perfectionibus*) which flow from him and can be found in his creatures, but which exist in him in an excellent manner (*secundum eminentiorem modum*) (*Summa Theologiae*, 1.13.3).

However, this solution is also subject to various objections. Firstly, in the sense in which we normally speak of causes and effects, it is not necessary that effects reflect the characteristics of their causes. This is often not the case: children do not always look like their parents, nor do statues look like their sculptors! Secondly, as we have already seen, the analogy of attribution allows too much: God is for example the Creator of our bodies, yet he is not corporeal. Thirdly, Aquinas' appeal to the analogy of proportionality makes vacuous the proposed likenesses between God and creatures. For it is unclear in what way God possesses the relevant characteristics. What could it mean on the basis of this kind of analogy to say that he has the characteristics *secundum eminentiorem modum*? Here too, it seems, agnosticism cannot be avoided: how can we, from our knowledge of earthly characteristics, draw conclusions about the characteristics which God possesses *secundum eminentiorem modum*? According to Aquinas, we cannot know the nature of God as he is in himself. We can, however, understand it in the way in which it is represented in the characteristics of his creatures (*secundum quod repraesentatur in perfectionibus creaturarum*) (*Summa Theologia*, 1.13.2). This does not help us any further as long as we cannot determine what the nature of this 'representation' might be.

These objections could be partly overcome if we interpret the
term 'cause' which Aquinas uses, not merely in its customary
sense of *causa efficiens* (efficient cause), but as 'cause' in the
Aristotelian sense of *causa finalis* (ideal or exemplar). God is not
only the *causa efficiens* (Creator) of the world; he is also the *causa
finalis* (ideal or exemplar) for his creatures. God's wisdom is the
perfect or ideal wisdom and as such the ultimate standard by
which we can judge the wisdom of his creatures. We are wise to
the extent that we approximate the wisdom of God. If we
interpret Aquinas' theory in this way, then the objections which
we have raised above come to stand in a different light. Firstly,
if God's characteristics (*perfectiones*) are to function as the
ultimate standard by which ours are to be measured, then it
must in some degree be possible for ours to approximate those of
God. But then there cannot be an absolute qualitative difference
between them. A *causa finalis* must necessarily have something in
common with that for which it is the ultimate standard of
perfection, whereas a *causa efficiens* need not have something in
common with its effects. Secondly, the analogy is only concerned
with *perfections* and not with all the characteristics of the
creature. God is for example wise, powerful, good, and so on,
but not corporeal. Corporality is presumably not one of the
perfections. Thirdly, the relationship between God's characteristics (as perfections) and those of human beings now becomes
clear in a way that it was not clear with the analogy of
proportionality: God's perfections relate to human characteristics (for example, God's wisdom to human wisdom) as an
ultimate standard relates to that which is measured by it. God's
wisdom is excellent (*secundum eminentiorem modum*) in the sense of
being exemplary.[15]

On the basis of this interpretation, the theory of Aquinas
becomes more attractive in some respects. However, it becomes
useless as the basis for natural theology. It would in fact be a
naturalistic fallacy to derive an ultimate standard from the

---

[15] For a helpful development of such a 'normative' interpretation of analogy, see Roger
White, 'Notes on analogical predication and speaking about God', in B.
Hebblethwaite and S. Sutherland (eds.), *The Philosophical Frontiers of Christian
Theology* (Cambridge, 1982), 197–226. See also sections 4.3 and 4.4 below.

entities which are to be measured by it. We can only know the extent and the sense in which creatures are good on the basis of our knowledge of God's goodness. However, we cannot infer God's goodness as ultimate standard from our knowledge of the creaturely goodness which is to be measured by it. God's perfections determine ours and not the other way around. In short: our knowledge of God's goodness, wisdom, and so forth is not to be derived from our knowledge of the world. On the one hand, it is clear that we speak about God with the *same* words that we use to speak about creatures. Our talk about God assumes therefore that there is indeed an *analogy* (common characteristics) between God (as ultimate standard) and creatures (who approximate this standard and are judged by it). On the other hand, this analogy does not offer a sufficient basis for a *natural theology*.

The fact that God created human beings in the way he did, having certain characteristics (including personal character-istics) in common with him, does not as such enable us to *infer* from the fact that we have these characteristics that God also has them. It does not help us if we relate the analogy to the assumption that effects always reflect the characteristics of their causes, and that the characteristics of God as Creator are therefore also reflected in his creatures. This assumption is in itself contentious. Nor does it help us to relate the analogy to the assumption that standards of perfection are always approxi-mated by the perfection of the entities which are judged by them. Inferring divine perfection from that of creatures would be a naturalistic fallacy.

4 *'Analogia fidei'*

Against the *analogia entis* of Thomas Aquinas, Karl Barth in his *Church Dogmatics* defends a theory known as *analogia fidei*.[16] Barth's theological starting point here is that we cannot acquire knowledge of God by ourselves. We can only know God when

[16] See his *Church Dogmatics*, II, 1, 237–43 (English edition, Edinburgh, 1957) where Barth discusses the problem of analogy in connection with the views of A. Quenstedt, the seventeenth-century Lutheran theologian.

God enables us to do so through his revelation. On the basis of this starting point, Barth rejects all natural theology and consequently the *analogia entis* as a basis for it.

However, Barth rejects the *analogia entis* only as a basis for natural knowledge of God but does not reject the analogy between God and us as a basis for our talk about God.[17] As G. C. Berkouwer points out, it is clear that for Barth the issue is not that of contesting the *analogia entis* with respect to the problem of analogical concepts in general, which is particularly relevant with respect to the Middle Ages, but the issue is the *analogia entis* (between God and creatures) in connection with our knowledge of God.[18]

In contrast to the view taken in his commentary on *The Epistle to the Romans*, Barth is here, like Aquinas, *not* defending an infinite qualitative difference between God and creatures. He does not deny that there are common (analogous) characteristics between God and us. Like Aquinas, Barth is also *not* defending an agnosticism such as Crombie's: we can achieve knowledge about which characteristics are common and thus we know what our words mean when we talk about God. In contrast to Aquinas, Barth rejects natural theology and the *analogia entis* as its foundation. *We only know* on the basis of God's revelation what characteristics God has in common with us. This knowledge is (as Barth asserts it in his discussion on Quenstedt) not 'calculable' or acquired apart from revelation by means of 'free recollection' from our knowledge of ourselves.

---

[17] On the interpretation defended by James Ross (see note 14 above), this also applies to Aquinas. On this interpretation, Aquinas' doctrine of analogy is a purely *semantic* theory and not an *epistemological* one.

[18] G. C. Berkouwer, *De Triomf der Genade in de Theologie van Karl Barth* (Kampen, 1954), 175. English translation: *The Triumph of Grace in the Theology of Karl Barth* (Grand Rapids, MI, 1956).

2.4 METAPHOR

1 The semantics of metaphor

We have now examined various possible answers to the question whether our human concepts are or are not applicable to God. Can we or can we not grasp the reality of God in human concepts? If we state the issue in this way, there are three possible answers. Firstly, an answer in terms of the infinite qualitative difference between God and the world: 'If we are going to speak about God with human words and concepts, we must be aware that every human word and concept falls short of that which we actually would like to say but cannot put into words: the reality of God. Every human word is, as such, inadequate for *this* reality, the reality of God' (Van Niftrik). Secondly, anthropomorphism: God is a fully human God. Therefore our human words and concepts can perfectly well be applied to him. Thirdly, the theory of analogy: God is partly like human persons (who are made in his image) and thus our human concepts are partly applicable and partly not applicable to the reality of God.

This way of stating the problem of analogy is in terms of the *names model* of language. In this model, words are names for concepts and concepts are mental representations which portray reality either completely, or only partly or not at all. Our human concepts and the words which name them apply only partly or not at all to God. The question is whether this model is adequate for the clarification of our use of analogical or metaphorical concepts.

The problem of analogy takes on a quite different form if we formulate it in terms of a *tools model*[19] of language, where

---

[19] The *names model* and the *tools model* are the two most important models in terms of which the relation between words, concepts and reality has been understood throughout the centuries. The names model is the most widespread and is to be found in the works of such divergent philosophers as Plato, Aristotle, Locke, Kant and the early Wittgenstein. According to this model concepts are mental representations or signs which correspond to things or to universals as the fundamental structures of reality and/or experience, while words are viewed as names for concepts and consequently also for the things and/or the universals. The word 'red', for example,

concepts are considered as forms of thought or mental capacities, and words as the tools by means of which we exercise
these capacities. The problem with metaphor is then not a
problem of the correspondence between words and (portrayed)
reality, but of the correspondence between *the use* of one and the
same word in two different conceptual contexts. Analogy
consists then not of a relationship between words and things,
but in the relationship of the *conceptual capacities* which are
expressed with the same word in different contexts.

Compare the use of the word 'see' in the statement 'I *saw* a
car on the road' with the use of the same word in the statements
'I *saw* a chance to do something about it', 'I *saw* the point of his
joke' and 'I *saw* a solution to his problem'. We are concerned
here with two *analogous uses* of the word 'see', in the language of
visual perception and in the language of *intellectual insight*. The
concepts (viewed as capacities), which are 'exercised' in two
different contexts with the very same word, are analogous but
not the same: the implications of the concept 'see' in relation to
visual perception are not *all* transferable to the context of
intellectual insight. It makes sense, for example, to ask: 'How
far away was the car when you saw it?' or 'Was the light good
enough to see the car?' Such questions would be absurd when
we are concerned with seeing the point of a joke or the chance
of solving a problem.

In similar fashion there are differences in the concepts 'see' in
the statements 'From the grandstand I could see everything
that happened on the field' and 'God sees everything'. Not all
the implications of the concept 'see' in the context of a spectator
on the grandstand can be transferred to the context of our
talking about the all-seeing eye of God. In this connection
Wittgenstein asked the rhetorical question: 'Are eyebrows

is a name for the concept 'red' and thus also for the colour 'red' to which this concept
corresponds. According to the tools model (advocated by Wittgenstein in his later
works) concepts are mental capacities that we exercise in our interaction with each
other in the world, while words are the tools by means of which we exercise these
capacities. The concept 'red' is here considered as a capacity to distinguish red
objects from objects which are not red, to point to red objects, to be able to say which
things are red, and so on, while the word 'red' is a tool with which we exercise this
capacity. For a more detailed discussion of the difference between these models, see
my *Theology and Philosophical Inquiry*, ch. 3. See also section 1.2 above.

going to be talked of in connection with the Eye of God?'[20] In summary: there is an *analogy* between the concept 'see' in relation to the spectator and the concept 'see' in relation to God. But these concepts are not identical.

When one word is used for two analogous concepts, the most common concept is usually called the 'literal' concept and the less common, the 'derived' or 'metaphorical' concept. Thus, for example, the use of the word *see* in relation to visual perception is literal and in relation to intellectual insight it is derived or metaphorical. This distinction is not absolute. It is not always clear which concept is literal and which derived. For example, the term 'make contact' is used when we speak about objects which are actually touching each other, and also when we talk about communication between people who are not actually touching each other. Which of these concepts is literal and which derived? In this connection shifts can take place, so that concepts which were once seen as derived have become so ordinary that they are now seen as literal. Metaphors 'die' and are experienced as having a literal meaning (for example, 'the *leg* of a chair'), while what was once a literal meaning may become uncommon and be seen as derived.

When the same word is used in a religious and in a non-religious context, it is not always the religious use that is derived or metaphorical.[21] Sometimes the religious concept is the most common and the non-religious concept appears to be the derived one (for example, if we use the word 'god' to call Mao 'the god of the Chinese'). Here too it is often not clear which concept is literal and which is derived. It is therefore wrong to assume that all concepts relating to God are in this sense metaphorical. Ultimately it is of less importance to determine which of the analogous concepts is literal and which is derived. It is much more important to determine which implications of the one are also valid for the other.

Summarizing, we can say that the problem of analogical (non-literal) concepts is not a problem concerned with the

[20] Ludwig Wittgenstein, *Lectures and Conversations on Aesthetics, Psychology and Religious Belief* (Oxford, 1966), 71.
[21] See in this connection Smart, *The Philosophy of Religion*, 65ff.

correspondence between words and things, but a problem concerned with the correspondence between concepts in different conceptual contexts of human life and thought. The questions which have to be answered here are: Which of the implications which are relevant in one context are also relevant in the other? Which implications of the concepts that we use in speaking about people are also valid for the parallel concepts which we use in speaking about God? And how is this to be established?

2 Parables

This issue can be explained in the light of the analysis which D. D. Evans gives of biblical parables.[22] Evans distinguishes three kinds of parables in the Bible. Firstly, the *exemplary parables*: stories or events or human actions which present examples of things that we should emulate or should avoid. Examples include the parable of the pharisee and the tax-gatherer (Luke 18: 9–14), the parable of the good Samaritan (Luke 10: 25–37) and the washing of the disciples' feet (John 13: 1–16). Secondly, *interpretative parables*: stories or events or human actions which provide interpretations of specific historic events (e.g. the crucifixion) or persons (e.g. Jesus) in terms of specific divine actions. Examples include the parable of the unjust tenants (Mark 12: 1–12) or the entry of Jesus into Jerusalem on Palm Sunday (Matthew 21: 1–11, cf. Zachariah 9: 9). Thirdly, *relational parables*: stories or events or human actions which illustrate in general the relationship between God and every human person. Examples include the parable of the prodigal son (Luke 15: 11–32) or the history of Hosea and Gomer (Hosea 3: 1).

In all these cases a parable *could* be a purported event, like the washing of the disciples' feet, the entry into Jerusalem and the history of Hosea and Gomer. But historicity is not necessary for a parable. A story can often fulfil the function of a parable just as well as a concrete event. Interpretative parables do have a

---

[22] D. D. Evans, *The Logic of Self-Involvement* (London, 1963), 220–5.

special relation to historical events, however, since, unlike the other kinds of parables, they provide an interpretation of a historical event, or a historical person.

In our present context the relational parables are especially relevant. These parables always involve four distinct points. Firstly: in certain circumstances people will ordinarily behave in this or that way with respect to someone else (e.g. a father on the return of his son will receive him with open arms); secondly: it is clear to us what reaction is appropriate to this action (e.g. the son should accept the forgiveness of his father with gratitude); thirdly: God is obviously quite different from other people – he is the Transcendent One; fourthly: our relation with God is analogous to the relation depicted in the parable, to the extent that it is clear what attitude we should adopt in relation to God.

Every parable has a single point, namely a practical message concerning the attitude which is appropriate with respect to God. It is in this respect that a parable differs from an allegory. Not all possible inferences are thus permitted. For example, in Luke 18: 1–8 the parable tells the story of an unjust judge, who is slow to act in helping a widow. The point of this parable is not that God is slow to help people, but that perseverance in prayer and trust are appropriate in relation to God. Which inferences are and which are not admissible in a specific parable depends on its relation with other parables. Thus, every parable should be 'weighed' against the other parables. They complement each other. In the history of doctrine, heresies often resulted from the fact that people drew the wrong conclusions from specific parables or images, and as a result came to conclusions which did not fit in with the implications of other, complementary images. Bethune-Baker gives a good example of this. He points out that

Arius seems, in part at least, to have been misled by a wrong use of analogy, and by mistaking description for definition. All attempts to explain the nature and relations of the Deity must largely depend on metaphor, and no one metaphor can exhaust those relations. Each metaphor can only describe one aspect of the nature or being of the Deity, and the inferences which can be drawn from it have their limits when they conflict with the inferences which can be truly drawn from other metaphors describing other aspects. From one point of view Sonship is a true description of the inner relations of the Godhead: from another point of view the title Logos describes them best. Each metaphor must be limited by the other. The title Son may obviously imply later origin and a distinction amounting to ditheism. It is balanced by the other title Logos, which implies co-eternity and inseparable union. Neither title exhausts the relations. Neither may be pressed so far as to exclude the other.[23]

In the Bible God is spoken of in *personal* terms. The same terms which are used to speak about human persons are also used for God. This does not mean that *all* implications which these terms have when we use them to speak about people also apply with respect to God.

When we use personal concepts with reference to God, it is often the gerundive implications of these concepts which are especially relevant.[24] In other words, we want to indicate the attitudes that are appropriate in relation to God in terms of the attitudes that are appropriate in relation to people. Even here there is of course a real difference. God is transcendent in the sense that the attitudes in relation to God go beyond those in relation to people. The glory, the authority and the faithfulness of God differ from these qualities in people in that they are unconditional or unlimited. The glory of God is different from that of people, in the sense that *unlimited* honour is fitting in relation to God; God's authority is unconditional and unlimited in the sense that there is no imaginable situation in which we could say: the authority of God is not valid here. God's faithfulness is unlimited in the sense that unconditional trust in God is fitting. There is indeed no imaginable situation in which we could say: Here God is no longer faithful and therefore is not to be trusted.

As in the case of relational parables, the personal concepts which are used in the Bible with respect to God, primarily

---

[23] J. F. Bethune-Baker, *An Introduction to the Early History of Christian Doctrine* (London, 1903), 160. Recent scholarship casts some doubt on Bethune-Baker's interpretation of Arius. However, this does not affect the point illustrated by the example.

[24] On gerundive terms, see my *Theology and Philosophical Inquiry*, 111, 119–29.

express the attitude or disposition that we are to adopt in relation to God. The description of God's factual nature or character is derived from this: God's factual characteristics are only known to us (and relevant from a religious point of view) to the extent that they are constitutive assumptions for the way of life that we are to adopt in relation to God.[25] The question of God's factual nature is therefore never an *existentially neutral* question which we can disconnect from the question about the way of life which we are to lead in the presence of God. The questions which believers ask about God's factual nature are never asked out of mere curiosity in the way in which they might out of curiosity ask questions about the factual nature of the world around them. As we have suggested above, we are able to know God *adequately* from his revelation. From God's revelation we can come to know both how we should act in relation to God, and how we should act *coram Deo* in relation to the world and each other. We can know no more about God's factual nature than what is necessary as the constitutive assumption for such a life *coram Deo*. For believers this is sufficient.

2.5 CONCEPTUAL MODELS

1 Metaphors and models

Metaphorical language or the use of metaphors is an essential feature of human thought in general. Every attempt to understand our experience of the world depends on a form of comparison: I understand X by comparing it to Y and by noticing that X is in some way or another like Y – even though I am fully aware that X differs from Y in many other respects. According to Sallie McFague,

a metaphor is seeing one thing *as* something else, pretending 'this' is 'that' because we do not know how to think or talk about 'this', so we use 'that' as a way of saying something about it. Thinking meta-

---

[25] See my paper on 'A dialogue of language-games', in V. Brümmer (ed.), *Interpreting the Universe as Creation: A Dialogue of Science and Religion* (Kampen, 1991), where I discuss this point more fully. See also my paper on 'Lyttkens on religious experience and transcendence', *Religious Studies*, 15 (1979), 221–5.

phorically means spotting a thread of similarity between two dissimilar
objects, events, or whatever, and using the better-known one as a way
of speaking about the lesser known.[26]

In the previous section we argued that this kind of metaphorical
thinking is fundamental in theology. We speak about God in
parables. In science too metaphors play a fundamental role.
Metaphorical comparisons are used in all scientific discoveries
and explanations. Thus Newton discovered something about
the moon by observing that the moon was like an apple which
fell from a tree to the ground near him – both being subject to
gravity. Naturally what the moon and an apple have in common
is very limited, but by observing that one crucial point of
agreement, Newton was able to discover why the moon
continued to circle the earth instead of shooting through space
in a straight line. In the previous section we showed how this
also holds for theological metaphors. The parables of Jesus each
make one single point and the images which are used in the
Bible to speak about God often rest on a very limited point of
similarity. We can call God a rock in order to indicate how
dependable God is, but that is the end of the similarity. Other
things that we can say about rocks do not apply to God.

In science, metaphors are sometimes used in a more extended
way by making them into *conceptual models*, that is, 'sustained
and systematic metaphors'[27] by means of which the behaviour
of physical phenomena can be systematically investigated and
explained. A phenomenon is investigated by means of a
systematic exploration of the extent to which it is similar to
another phenomenon. In this way the behaviour of gases is
studied by systematically comparing this behaviour with that of
billiard balls on a billiard table, and by applying the kind of
mathematical calculations used in explaining the interaction of
the balls to the interaction between the gas particles in a gas
container. Obviously, gases are quite different from billiard

[26] Sallie McFague, *Metaphorical Theology* (London, 1983), 15. McFague's book gives a
more detailed analysis than is possible here of the function of metaphors and models
in religion and theology. See also my article on 'Metaphorical thinking and
systematic theology', *Nederlands Theologisch Tijdschrift*, 43 (1989), 213–28, and my
What Are We Doing When We Pray? (London, 1984), 150ff.

[27] Max Black, *Models and Metaphors* (Ithaca, NY, 1962), 236.

balls, but much can be achieved in explaining the behaviour of gases by making use of the billiard ball model. Much can also be achieved by explaining the behaviour of rays of light in terms of waves or in terms of moving particles.[28]

In theology too some metaphors are systematically developed as conceptual models. Obviously, not all metaphors lend themselves to this equally well.[29] We can call God a rock in order to indicate his dependability, but that is the end of the comparison. This metaphor cannot be usefully developed further into a systematic model of talking about God. In the Bible and the theological tradition, God is spoken about as a person, and our relationship with God is viewed as a personal relation. These metaphors have proved to be fruitful in their systematic development as models. Ultimately God is of course not like other persons and our relationship with God is not like our relationship with each other. The fact that we can get a long way by using personal models in our thinking about God does not mean that these models do not reach their limits at certain points, especially when they lead to implications that contradict doctrines concerning God which we are not prepared to reject. The conceptual problems with which philosophical theology concerns itself often take the following form: How far can we develop specific theological models (for example, the personal models) without their coming into conflict with doctrines which we are not willing to give up?

2 A games-theoretical matrix

The chapters that follow will be devoted to an analysis of four interconnected examples of this kind of problem in relation to the use of personal models in theology. Before we can discuss these problems, however, it is necessary to give a preliminary schematic indication of the nature of personal models and of the

[28] See Ian G. Barbour, *Myths, Models and Paradigms* (London, 1974), 30 (on the billiard ball model) and 71 (on the wave and particles model in the theory of light). Barbour's book provides a useful comparison between the use of models in science and in theology. For such a comparison, see also Janet Martin Soskice, *Metaphor and Religious Language*, 3rd edn (Oxford, 1988), 97–117.

[29] For an elaboration of this point in connection with Old Testament theology, see Terence E. Fretheim, *The Suffering of God* (Philadelphia, PA, 1984), 10–12.

way in which they can be used for structuring our thinking about our relationship with God. We will do this with the aid of the following matrix from games theory:

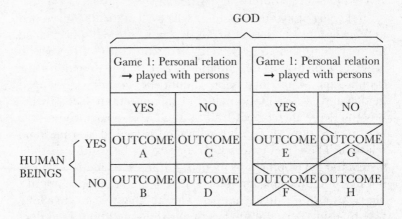

Two alternative games are to be distinguished in this matrix: Game 1 and Game 2. In Game 1 the relationship between the players is a personal relationship: both players are persons, who can choose whether to say Yes or No to each other. There are four possible outcomes in this game, A, B, C and D. In Game 2 the relationship between the players is a purely causal one: only one of the players is a person, who can say Yes or No. The other is a robot programmed to says Yes in response to a Yes, and No in response to a No. There are only two possible outcomes here, E or H.

In his relation with us, God decides which game (or which kind of world) is to be the relevant context for our interaction with him. If God wants outcome A more than anything else, that is, a personal relationship of mutual love, he chooses Game 1 and he says Yes as an opening move: God offers us his love.

In Game 1 there are now two responses open to us: we can choose outcome A by saying Yes and reciprocating God's love. We can also choose outcome B by saying No and rejecting God's love. We have every reason to choose A, and yet we choose B: the 'impossible possibility' of sin.

If we were to say Yes and return God's love, then God will

maintain his Yes and guarantee outcome A. We can count on it that God will not withdraw his Yes and reject those who come to him (outcome C).

In response to our rejection of his love (outcome B), there are three options open to God. He can firstly withdraw his Yes and reject us (outcome D). In this way we are denied the possibility of salvation. The consequence is the death of the sinner. God does not choose this possibility, because 'I have no desire for the death of the wicked. I would rather that a wicked man should mend his ways and live' (Ezekiel 33: 11).

Secondly, God could prevent us from saying No and *cause* everybody to say Yes (outcome E) or cause some people to say Yes and others to say No (outcomes E and H respectively). In order to achieve this, however, God has to abandon Game 1 and go over to Game 2. In this case we are no longer persons but 'senseless stocks and blocks'.[30] Furthermore, outcome A cannot now be achieved and God must be satisfied with outcome E instead. Given that God is not a Promethean manipulator, he finds no satisfaction in outcome E and thus does not choose this move. 'Neither by force of arms nor by brute strength, but by my Spirit! says the Lord of Hosts' (Zechariah 4: 6).

Thirdly, he can maintain his offer of salvation in the hope that we may withdraw our No and eventually say Yes, so that outcome A will as yet be achieved. To this end God can reveal his love to us in his Son and, through his Spirit, *inspire* us to return his love. Being inspired by the Spirit is not a form of *causal manipulation* but a motivating action which acknowledges our status as *persons*. In this way outcome A remains open, in contrast to outcome E, where we are turned into sinlessly programmed robots.[31]

These various possible outcomes entail different kinds of eschatology. If we were to view our relationship with God in terms of Game 2 instead of Game 1, we would have an eschatology of strict deterministic predestination, which could be either universalistic (outcome E for everyone), or a form of

[30] *The Canons of Dordt*, ch. 3/4, art. 16. See also chapter 3 below.
[31] For the distinction between causal manipulation and motivating inspiration, see section 3.6 below.

double predestination (outcome E for some and H for others). If God indeed chooses Game 1 and responds to our No by maintaining his Yes in order to keep open the possibility that we should repent, the question arises: How long does God keep this possibility open? There are two possible answers here.

On the one hand, it could be argued that God will not accept a No from anyone, and therefore holds open the possibility of repentance for *every* individual until that individual has turned to God. Not even death would cut off the possibility of repentance in this case. Outcome B would remain open to everybody after death, until every individual turns to God and outcome A is achieved in the end for everyone. Hell is then a place of purification (or purgatory) where people stay until they have turned to God.[32] This option implies a universalism: ultimately everyone will achieve salvation, nobody is excluded for all eternity. This means that God does not accept the final consequence of the fact that he has made us persons. The freedom required in order to be a person includes the freedom to reject the love of God permanently and decisively. In this case, therefore, God would ultimately fail to take the rejection of his love seriously. Another possibility is to propose that the freedom of a person also entails the freedom to reject salvation permanently and to choose eternal death. In this case God accepts our No in the long run and does not keep the possibility of salvation open, so that outcome D can be achieved. The implication of this is the doctrine of the annihilation of the godless. Their death is final, given that they have no part in the resurrection.[33]

The various options in the games-theoretical matrix also entail different forms of salvation: outcome A or outcome E. Clearly God attaches so much more value to outcome A than to outcome E that he lets us live in a world such as ours (Game 1) in which outcome A is possible and not in a deterministic paradise (Game 2) in which men are sinlessly programmed

---

[32] See for example Friedrich Schleiermacher, *Der christliche Glaube, nach den Grundsatzen der evangelischen Kirche in Zusammenhange dargestellt*, 7th edn (Berlin, 1960), English translation: *The Christian Faith* (Edinburgh 1968), §163.

[33] See for example Martin Luther, *Werke* (Weimar edition), XVII, 235 and XLVIII, 155.

robots rather than persons, and only outcome E is possible. In choosing Game 1, God takes the risk of our rejecting his love (outcome B). This in turn entails the possibility of evil in the world.

3 Conceptual problems

Although this games-theoretical matrix is rather schematic, it does enable us to distinguish the most important aspects of the use of a personal model for our relationship with God. Is this kind of model adequate for thinking about our relationship with God, or does further development of it conflict with fundamental doctrines of the Christian tradition which we are not prepared to give up? In the following chapters we will examine four interconnected problems of this kind and see whether the personal model can be so developed that these problems can be answered in a satisfactory way.

The first problem is concerned with human freedom. If our salvation lies in a personal relationship with God (outcome A), that assumes that we are also free to reject God's offer of grace, and thus also that our salvation is partly dependent on our own free choice not to resist God's grace. Is this not in conflict with the classical doctrine of *sola gratia* which maintains that salvation depends on God alone and not on us? How 'irresistible' is the grace of God?

The second problem is concerned with the freedom of God. A personal model implies not only that we are free in relation to God, but that God is also free in relation to us. Does this mean that God (like us) is free to do evil? Is that not in conflict with the classical doctrine of the *impeccabilitas Dei*, which claims not only that he *is* not, but also that he *cannot* be the author of evil?

The third problem is concerned with the relation between divine and human agency. If God and human persons are free agents in relation to each other, how is their agency related? According to John Burnaby, 'the power of God's love takes effect in human history in no other way than through the wills and actions of men in whom that love has come to dwell'.[34] Does

[34] John Burnaby, 'Christian prayer', in A. R. Vidler (ed.), *Soundings* (Cambridge, 1962), 232–3.

not this theory of 'double agency' either deny the freedom of human persons by turning them into the tools of divine action, or limit the freedom of God by making his agency dependent on the free decisions of human agents?

The fourth problem is concerned with the existence of evil. We have shown how a personal model is the basis of the traditional theodicy known as the free will defence: evil in the world is the consequence of the fact that God chooses outcome A, and thus also accepts the risk of sin. Evil is the price that we have to pay for the possibility of this outcome. The question is often asked whether this price is not too high. Ivan Karamazov, for example, considered the price for outcome A as much too high.

Too high a price has been placed on harmony. We cannot afford to pay so much for admission. And therefore I hasten to return my ticket of admission. And indeed, if I am an honest man, I'm bound to hand it back as soon as possible. This I am doing. It is not God that I do not accept, Alyosha. I merely most respectfully return him the ticket.[35]

The possibility of having a personal relationship with God involves a risk that is not worth all the misery in the world. So he ends up in rebellion against God. Is this not the reaction of many people who are bowed down under suffering? In short, is not a theodicy based on a personal model so morally insensitive that it fails to offer a consolation to human beings in their hour of need?

The use of a personal model for conceiving of our relationship with God has implications for *all* aspects of Christian doctrine. In the following chapters we will however concentrate on these four issues rather than try to discuss the implications of personal models for all aspects of Christian doctrine. Such a complete discussion would require another book or books, and is not necessary for our present purposes.[36] The four issues we will discuss form a coherent whole and are central to the use of personal models in the doctrine of God. A discussion of these

[35] Fyodor Dostoyevsky, *The Brothers Karamazov* (Harmondsworth, 1982), 287.
[36] For an analysis of some further problems arising from the use of personal models in Christian doctrine, see my *What Are We Doing When We Pray?*

issues from this point of view will provide a sufficient basis for our epilogue in which we will return to the issues raised in the previous chapter: what is the role of philosophical reflection in dealing with theological issues such as those to which we now turn?

CHAPTER 3

Can we resist the grace of God?

3.1 IRRESISTIBILITY

Towards the end of section 2.4 we suggested that the Christian way of life can best be described as a life lived *coram Deo*, in the presence of God. How we conceive of the relationship to God is therefore of significance for our view on the nature of life within this relationship. The question about the nature of our relationship with God is therefore fundamental, not only for theology, but also for the way of life of a Christian. Which of the relationships that people have with each other is the most adequate for us to use as a conceptual model for thinking about our relationship with God? In the Christian tradition there have been many different views on this, with far-reaching consequences for both doctrine and life.

These differences can be well illustrated with reference to the traditional theological claim that it is impossible for us to resist the grace of God, since different relation-models with reference to the relation between God and human beings entail different views about the nature of this irresistibility. The claim that God's grace is irresistible seems to be a necessary corollary of the view that salvation is by grace alone. If we were able to resist God's grace, it would seem that our salvation also depends on our not resisting it, and that we can therefore claim some of the credit ourselves instead of saying *soli Deo gloria!* and giving all the credit to God. For this reason the irresistibility of grace has in some form or another been explicitly defended or implicitly presupposed by many eminent theologians from the church fathers to the present day. A standard example of an explicit defence of this doctrine is that of the Synod of Dordt in 1618–19 where Reformed divines from all over Europe upheld this doctrine against the doubts raised by the followers of Jacob Arminius. In this chapter we will inquire which relation-model is presupposed in the views of the Dordt divines as expressed in the Canons of the Synod of Dordt and trace the implications of reinterpreting their views in terms of alternative relation-models.

Is it *impossible* for us to resist God's offer of salvation? Is grace actually *irresistible*? If we analyse the question further, then it appears to be difficult to answer on account of its generality. It is not precisely clear what is being asked, given the fact that modal concepts such as 'possible', 'impossible' and 'necessary' (= 'impossible not to') have no unequivocal meaning. It is therefore much more sensible to ask: in what sense of 'impossible' is it impossible to resist the grace of God? Because the theologians at Dordt failed to take this aspect of the question into account, their followers have often talked at cross purposes when this problem was being discussed. It is theologically important to state the question clearly, given that there is a link between the kind of 'impossibility' which is being postulated and the view we take of the relationship between God and human persons. Different ideas about this relationship imply different ways in which it is impossible to reject God's offer of salvation.

For our present purposes it would be useful to distinguish the following four senses of 'impossible': 1. conceptually impossible, 2. factually impossible, 3. normatively impossible and 4. rationally impossible. Let us see which view of our relationship with God is implied when we interpret the doctrine of irresistibility in terms of these four senses of 'impossible'.

3.2 CONCEPTUAL IMPOSSIBILITY

In modal logic a distinction is sometimes made between conceptually impossible (i.e. impossible by definition) and logically impossible.[1] It is *logically* impossible to do something if the assertion that it has been done is a contradiction, no matter how the terms in the assertion are defined. Thus it is for example logically impossible to resist an irresistible force, because it is a contradiction to maintain that someone does that – no matter how we define the term 'resist'. In this sense it is not logically impossible to resist the grace of God, since we could define the terms of this claim in such a way that it would not be contradictory to claim that someone does so. There would only be a contradiction involved if we were to *define* 'grace' as an irresistible force. In that case it would be conceptually impossible (or impossible by definition) to claim that the grace of God can be resisted.

Whether something is or is not conceptually impossible depends thus on the *definition* of our terms. A definition is a conceptual rule by which we specify the range of the concept to which we want to apply the defined term. We use such a conceptual rule to set out the conditions under which we will recognize something as falling within the extension of the relevant term. We use a definition of the term 'grace' to state the conditions under which we are prepared to recognize something as an exercise of grace. If, for example, we include in the definition that grace is an irresistible force, then we exclude *by definition* that something can count as an exercise of grace when in fact it can be resisted.

Every attempt to interpret the grace of God in this way as irresistible *by definition* has to face two difficulties. Firstly, this position has the remarkable consequence that it cannot count as an exercise of grace when God reveals himself to people or calls them to repentance and they ignore the revelation or refuse the call. Let us illustrate this point by means of some examples.

---

[1] See for example D. Paul Snyder, *Modal Logic and Its Applications* (New York, 1971), 166ff.

In the Canons of Dordt (chapter 3/4, article 4) it is proposed (with reference to Romans 1 : 18ff) that 'there remain, however, in man since the fall, the glimmerings of natural light, whereby he retains some knowledge of God'. Instead of 'using it aright', man is such that he 'in various ways renders it wholly polluted, and holds it back in unrighteousness'. In the context of this view, the proposition that God's grace is by definition irresistible would imply that the fact that God makes himself known to people in this manner cannot be considered as grace. This conclusion could be avoided by making a distinction between general grace and saving grace. Only the latter would then be irresistible *by definition*. In Romans 1 the reference is to general grace, which is certainly grace, albeit that it is 'held back in unrighteousness'.

A counter-example is that of Augustine. He had a believing mother who confronted him from his earliest years with the saving message of Christ. Augustine was not encountering here the general grace of Romans 1, but the special grace of the gospel. But this was not enough to bring him to repentance. It was only much later in his life that he came to repent and then described his path to salvation as a long-lasting attempt to escape from the message of salvation. Is this not an example of someone who for a large part of his life was engaged in resisting the saving grace of Christ? This example might be dealt with by claiming that saving grace is often manifested in a cumulative process and that in the end Augustine did come to repentance, and thus was not able to resist the process *in its entirety*. From that point of view there is thus no question here of resisting saving grace.

Much more problematic, however, are counter-examples such as that of Ahab. God sent Elijah repeatedly to call Ahab to repentance – but Ahab did not repent, not even in the end. Just as in Augustine's case, we are not here concerned with general grace but with a specific call to repentance through a prophet of God. Unlike the case of Augustine, the call to Ahab remained unanswered, even in the long run. The only possible conclusion from the point of view of those who would maintain that (saving) grace is by definition irresistible, is that this call from the prophet of God to Ahab was not an act of divine grace. But what was it then? A sort of cat and mouse game with Ahab? It is clear that the Dordt divines were aware of this dilemma and clearly rejected the view that God's message of salvation should ever be a mockery. For that reason they make very clear (chapter 3/4, article 8) that 'as many as are called by the gospel are unfeignedly called; for God hath most earnestly and truly declared in his Word what will be acceptable to him, namely, that all who are called should comply with the invitation'. That the authenticity of this call should apply not only with respect to those who accept it, is clear from article 9 where it is expressly stated that many of 'those who are called by the ministry of the Word refuse to come and be converted'. In short, the Dordt divines clearly draw back from the consequences of the view that grace is *conceptually* (or by definition) irresistible.

A second difficulty with this position is the following. Conceptual rules have implications. If we accept a conceptual rule, we are obliged to accept its further implications as well. We will presently show that all talk about our relationship to God as a personal relationship (that is, a relationship between persons) also rests on the assumption that it is possible in a certain sense to say 'no' to God. If we rule out this possibility by definition, we also exclude by implication the possibility that our relationship with God could be a personal relationship. We will come back to this presently.

3.3 FACTUAL IMPOSSIBILITY

If we do not exclude the possibility of certain actions by definition, this does not entail that we therefore have to consider them to be *factually* possible. It is not a contradiction to maintain that someone will break a piece of iron with his hands or will walk across the ceiling without assistance, or that a drug addict can stop using drugs without withdrawal therapy. Yet these things are in fact impossible, not on account of the way in which we define our terms, but on account of the actual structure of reality. Should we propose that the grace of God is such an overwhelming force that it is factually impossible for us to resist it? There are two considerations that can be brought against this proposal.

Firstly, given that examples such as those of Augustine and Ahab are not ruled out by definition, they remain as genuine counter-examples. We cannot maintain that an event is factually impossible if genuine examples can be brought forward where it occurs. Examples such as these form in themselves a decisive argument against the proposition that grace is factually irresistible. It is therefore understandable that this is put forward in the Five Arminian Articles of 1610 as a decisive argument against the doctrine of irresistibility: 'But as respects the mode of the operation of this grace, it is not irresistible, inasmuch as it is written concerning many, that they have resisted the Holy Ghost. Acts 7, and elsewhere in many places.'

A second difficulty with the claim that grace is factually irresistible is that to which we have already alluded above: the accompanying implication that our relationship with God is not personal, but a purely causal relationship. This requires further clarification. As was emphasized in the games-theoretical matrix in the previous chapter, a personal relationship is a relationship between *persons*. A person is by definition an agent, that is, someone who takes the initiative in what he or she does. In this respect there is a difference between the acts that someone performs and the events that happen to him or her. Thus *jumping* off the roof is an act, and *falling* off the roof is an event that happens to someone.

In this connection we could propose that with acts, in contrast to events, the free choice of the agent is by definition a necessary although not a sufficient condition for the act to take place. In this proposal the following points are of importance. Firstly, to be freely chosen is part of the definition of an act. If no choice is possible, we do not speak of someone's act, but of an event that happened to him or her. Secondly, a choice is by definition *avoidable*, and in this sense is free. The choice to do A thus always implies the ability not to do A. If someone is not able to avoid doing A, we cannot say that he or she *chooses* to do A, given that it is then something that unavoidably happens to him or her. Thirdly, the choice of the agent is one of the *necessary*

conditions for his or her act to take place. If the agent chooses
otherwise, then the act does not take place. Fourthly, the choice
of the agent is not a *sufficient* condition for the act to take place.
An agent cannot do something simply by choosing to do it. His
or her actual situation must make it possible to realize the
choice. Sartre would say that our freedom is always a *concrete*
freedom, that is, freedom only with respect to the concrete
possibilities that are available to us in our actual situation.[2]
Fifthly, the sufficient condition for the act to take place is
therefore the choice of the agent plus the given possibilities of
realizing the choice. If one of the two conditions is absent, the
act does not take place.

Given that the choice of an agent is a *necessary* condition for his
or her act, one person can never be the *complete* cause of the act
of another person. To be a complete cause, he or she would also
have to cause the choice of the other person, in which case the
other would no longer be the initiator and thus no longer the
agent. Given that the choice of the agent is not a *sufficient*
condition for his or her act, it is quite possible that one person
can be a *contributory* cause of another's action.[3] Also, although
one person cannot make the choice for another, he or she can
certainly create the conditions for the other to be able to realize
his or her choice. One person can also offer motives or reasons
for another to make a specific choice. Reasons are not causes,
and the other will always have to decide for him- or herself
whether the reasons given are a sufficient motive for the act in
question. In this sense the other person is, even in this case, the
initiator of his or her own act.

In the light of this analysis we can distinguish two senses of the
term 'freedom'[4] which we might call the freedom of ability and
the freedom of will. We can only talk of an act when the agent
is in both senses free to carry out the act. Someone has the
freedom of ability if his or her concrete situation provides the

---

[2] On this point, see my *Theology and Philosophical Inquiry* (London, 1981), 120–1.
[3] See in this connection R. M. Chisholm, *Person and Object* (London, 1976), 66–9.
[4] This distinction is analogous to that of Augustine between an exercise of power and
an exercise of the will. See chapter 53 of his treatise *De Spiritu et Littera*. For an
illuminating, but slightly different development of this distinction, see Antony Flew,
'Freedom and human nature', *Philosophy*, 66 (1991), 53–63.

actual possibility for carrying out the act. Without the freedom of ability no act is possible. Someone has the *freedom of will* if the given possibilities are not unavoidable events which will be realized whether or not the agent decides to bring them about. Without the freedom of will, he or she does not have the initiative, and we do not speak of an act but of an event that happens to him or her.

For the realization of a *personal relationship* the initiative of *both* partners in the relationship is necessary. Given that both partners in such a relationship are persons, both have by definition the freedom of will, by which it must be *factually possible* for both of them to say 'no' to the other and so to prevent the relationship coming into existence. It is only by means of the 'yes' of one partner that the other receives the freedom of ability to realize the relationship. In this respect personal relationships are symmetrical and differ from purely causal relationships, which are asymmetrical, because only one partner (the cause) can be the initiator. The other partner in a purely causal relationship is an object of causal manipulation and therefore lacks the freedom of will to be able to say 'no' with respect to what happens to him or her.

If our relationship to God is a personal relationship, this assumes on the one hand that God is a person. The relationship can only be brought about if God chooses it freely. It is not unavoidable for God as a person to enter into a personal relationship with us. The implication of this is that if our salvation is to be found in a personal relationship with God, we cannot achieve salvation by ourselves. We lack the freedom of ability, given that in a personal relationship we are by definition dependent for this freedom on Another with whom we enter into the relationship.

On the other hand, a personal relationship with God assumes that the human partner also remains a person in the relationship and that his or her free choice is equally a necessary condition for the relationship to be brought about. God can make it possible for us to enter into the relationship. He can even provide reasons which will motivate us to choose to enter into the relationship. But God cannot bring about our choice without it ceasing to be ours.[5] By definition a *personal* relationship with God cannot be factually unavoidable for the human partner. For this reason the doctrine of factual irresistibility excludes a personal relationship between God and human persons.

We have argued that a personal relationship is symmetrical in the sense that it can only be achieved by the free choice of both partners. In this respect a personal relationship with God is also symmetrical. On another level, however, the relationship is not symmetrical, given that we are only persons because God has made us so. It is also possible for God to deny us the freedom of will and to treat us as objects of his causal manipulation. In terms of our games-theoretical matrix: it is God who decides that we are to play Game 1 rather than Game 2. If he were to decide on Game 2, the consequence would be that our relationship with him would not be personal but purely causal. In summary: Grace is factually resistible given that we are persons – but we have God to thank and not ourselves for the fact *that* we are persons. In this sense we receive not only the freedom of ability from God, but also the freedom of will.[6]

On the question of whether our relationship with God is personal or causal, the Canons of Dordt adopt a remarkably ambivalent position. On the one hand, the factual resistibility of grace is unambiguously rejected, and grace is spoken of in purely causal terms as a power which operates on our will and fills it with new capacities.[7] There is no question of a personal choice on our part. On the other hand, it is explicitly denied that this should imply that we are objects of causal manipulation rather than persons. 'But as man by the fall did not cease to be a creature endowed with understanding and will...so also this grace of regeneration does not treat men as senseless stocks and blocks, nor take away their will and its properties, neither does violence thereto...' (chapter 3/4, article 16).

It strikes me that the difficulties here have their source in the fact that the Dordt theologians did not view human salvation in terms of a personal *relationship* with God but in terms of a reborn

---

[5] See Augustine, *De Spiritu et Littera*, ch. 54.   [6] See ibid., chs. 58 and 60.
[7] See for example ch. 3/4, arts. 11, 12 and 14 and objections 6, 7 and 8.

condition in us. The only question then concerns the *cause* of this condition: is it God or us, grace or human will? This way of stating the question leaves no room for the factual possibility of rejecting grace, and therefore also has as a consequence that we are made into objects of causal manipulation. The Dordt theologians understandably drew back from this consequence of their own way of stating the question.

3.4 NORMATIVE IMPOSSIBILITY

If our relationship to God is to be a personal relationship, then it must be *factually* possible for us to refuse to enter into it. However, this does not mean that there are not other senses of 'impossible' in terms of which it is impossible for us, precisely within such a personal relationship with God, to say 'no' to God's grace. There are here two options which in turn fit in with two different ways of understanding the personal relationship with God. If we interpret the relationship in legal terms as an agreement of rights and duties, it is normatively impossible for us to resist grace. If we see the relationship in terms of a relationship of fellowship or love, it is rationally impossible to resist grace. Let us examine these two options further.[8]

One form that personal relationships often have is that of an *agreement of rights and duties*. An example of this sort of relationship is an agreement between an employer and an employee in which the employer is committed to pay the employee a wage in exchange for services which the employee is obliged to perform for the employer. The following aspects are important in this sort of relationship. Firstly, it is a personal relationship given that the partners in the relationship are both persons and the relationship only comes about if both partners agree to it. Neither of the partners can bring about such a relationship without the agreement of the other. Secondly, each partner enters the relationship for his or her own benefit: the employer does it for the sake of the services which the employee provides,

---

[8] For further discussion of the implications of this distinction for the nature of the restoration of a broken relationship with God as this is addressed in the doctrine of atonement, see my paper on 'Atonement and reconciliation', in *Religious Studies* (forthcoming, 1992). See also section 6.4 below.

and the employee for the sake of the wages that he or she receives from his or her employer. Thirdly, the agreement determines the rights and obligations of the partners with respect to each other: the employee is entitled to the wage which the employer is obliged to give him or her; the employer is entitled to the services which the employee is obliged to provide for him or her. Fourthly, this kind of relationship is the context within which we can speak about merit and reward, guilt and punishment. By fulfilling your obligations within the relationship, you *merit* the *reward* to which you have a right. The employee earns his or her reward for performing the services he or she is obliged to perform. By not doing what you are obliged to do, you become *guilty* of failing in your duty and as *punishment* you could be deprived of the reward to which you would otherwise be entitled.

In the Bible the relationship between God and us is often described as a covenant relationship. This covenant relationship is sometimes interpreted on the analogy of an agreement of rights and duties in the sense described above. God offers us heavenly salvation in return for good works. By our good works we can *earn* salvation as reward. By failing to do good works we can forfeit our right to salvation and become *guilty*, and as punishment be denied the promised salvation. The doctrine of supererogatory good works could be taken as an extension of this model. We are concerned here with two kinds of good works: those works which we are obliged to do under the covenant agreement and supererogatory good works which we are permitted but not obliged to perform. Our covenant agreement with God obliges us only to the first category. It is however possible for us to earn an extra reward by doing the supererogatory good works. This reward can then serve to wipe out the debt that we run up by failing to do the obligatory good works.

In this kind of model salvation is a reward from God that can be earned by us through doing good works. It is factually possible for us to reject this offer by refusing to do the good works. But in a *legal* or *normative* sense it is not possible for us to reject this offer. It is not possible because it is *forbidden* by the terms of the agreement. Something that is forbidden is not *factually* impossible – even though it is ruled out from a normative point of view as being contrary to the agreement.

It is understandable that the Dordt divines could not accept this model for our relation with God because of the theology of merit which it entails. In order to eliminate every implication of human merit, they fell back on a causal model. In this model human salvation can in no way be earned – it is only to be realized through God's grace. In fact, using a causal model is the most radical way of denying that we can perform *meritorious acts*, because in terms of this model it is impossible for us to perform *any acts* at all, since we here cease to be agents and become objects of causal manipulation instead.

Apart from the difficulties discussed above with respect to this causal model, there are two more difficulties which arise when we exclude a theology of merit in this way. If we lack the ability to perform any acts, we certainly cannot earn any rewards by performing meritorious acts. But nor can we incur any debt by failing to perform such acts. Both *reward* and *debt* are related to acts that we do or fail to do, but not to events that happen to us. To exclude reward by the use of a causal model implies that all talk of debt and guilt will also be excluded. However, the Dordt divines were not willing to accept this implication of their causal model.[9]

Furthermore, if our relationship with God is a purely causal relationship, then God is the only *agent* in the relationship and thus by definition the only one who can claim merit for bringing about our salvation. But as the *only* agent, he is also by definition the only one who can be guilty if salvation is not achieved. If God is the only 'author', he is also the only one who can be the 'author of evil'. This implication of the causal model was equally unacceptable for the Synod of Dordt.[10]

In summary: interpreting our relationship with God in terms of an agreement of rights and duties entails a theology of merit. If we wish to avoid this implication by means of a causal view of our relationship with God, we make use of a drastic conceptual

---

[9] See for example ch. 1, art. 5 and ch. 2, art. 6.
[10] See for example ch. 1, art. 5 and the conclusion.

remedy which in turn involves a number of unacceptable implications. The question is now whether we could find an alternative model which is both personal, and therefore avoids the difficulties of a causal model, but on the other hand also avoids the theology of merit involved in a model of rights and duties. If it is neither factually impossible to resist grace, nor merely impossible in a normative sense, in what other sense could it be impossible?

3.5 RATIONAL IMPOSSIBILITY

Not all personal relationships are agreements of rights and duties in the above sense. There are also other relationships possible between persons, for example relationships of fellowship or love.[11] There are four aspects of these relationships which are important with reference to our relationship with God. Firstly, relationships based on love are relationships of reciprocal identification. Secondly, the partners in this relationship cannot compel each other to reciprocate their love, nor can they, thirdly, earn such reciprocation. Fourthly, it is impossible in the sense of being unreasonable within the relationship for one partner to reject the love of the other. Let us explain these four points in turn.

Relationships of love are in the first place relationships of *reciprocal identification*. Each partner in the relationship identifies with the other by making the interest of the other his or her own, and by pursuing this as his or her own interest. In this respect our relationship with God is comparable to a love relationship. God identifies himself with us by himself becoming human and making the human lot his own on the cross. By means of this identification God makes our salvation his own concern. On the other hand, in such a relation we can also identify with God by seeking his honour and glory as our own concern.

Secondly, given that a love relationship is a relationship between persons, it can only be achieved if each of the partners *freely* identifies with the other. By definition I cannot *compel*

---

[11] For some illuminating remarks on 'the logic of love', see J. R. Lucas, *Freedom and Grace* (London, 1976), especially chs. 2, 3, 7 and 8. See also section 6.4 below.

someone else to return my love. In this, love differs from sex. Sexual desires can be aroused in the other causally, but the love of the other can only be freely given. For this reason it remains factually possible to reject the love of another by refusing to return it.

In this respect too our relationship to God can be compared to a love relationship. We cannot compel God to love us. God remains free in his love. Likewise, God cannot compel us to reciprocate his love for us, since in that case our response by definition could not be love. That is why it was factually possible for Augustine for a long time to resist God's offer of love.

In the third place, the love of another *cannot be earned*. In a love relationship I pursue your interests because I have made them into my own interests by identifying with you. I do not pursue your interests in order to earn your loving response. This is where a love relationship differs from an agreement of rights and duties which we enter for the sake of earning rewards from one another.

Also in this respect our relationship to God can be compared to a love relationship. God's love cannot be earned: not because the price is too high or our exertion too feeble, but because it is love, and by definition love cannot be earned nor given away unearned. We simply cannot talk about love in terms of rewards which might or might not be merited.[12] God does not try to 'earn' our love with his offer of salvation. He wants us to love him because we identify with him, and not on account of what we can receive from him. If we love heaven instead of God, then our efforts are directed towards our own interests and we fail to identify ourselves with the interests of God.

In the fourth place, it is *rationally impossible* for someone who identifies in love with another to reject the love of the other. I am enabled to enter a love *relationship* with you only because you freely bestow this possibility on me by reciprocating my love and in so doing establishing the relationship for me to enter. Your response can be neither compelled nor obliged because, as

[12] See Lucas, *Freedom and Grace*, ch. 2.

we have shown, love cannot be forced nor can it be earned. Therefore everyone who identifies in love with someone else experiences the love of the other as a freely bestowed *favour* which the other is neither compelled nor obliged to give. It is unreasonable to reject what you experience as a favour. Gratitude is the only reasonable response from someone who is conscious of being favoured in this way.

This kind of rational impossibility applies to the believer in the strongest form in relation to God. If I am a believer, I look upon my life as life lived within the context of such a loving relationship with God. Since the very possibility for me to live my life in this way depends on the fact that God freely loved me first, living in the love of God remains an unmerited favour. Viewed from this perspective, it is therefore rationally impossible for me to reject the love of God.

The impossibility of rejecting a favour is similar to the impossibility of acting against your conscience. In both cases we are not concerned with a factual impossibility, nor with a merely normative impossibility, but with something that is impossible on account of its unreasonableness. When, as has been reported, Martin Luther concluded his defence at the Diet of Worms with the words 'Here I stand, I *cannot* do otherwise', he was not asserting the 'factual' impossibility of denying his own beliefs. He was not like a drug addict who states that he is unable to kick the habit. It would not have been in keeping with his argument if he had said: 'I have often tried, but unfortunately I have never been able to succeed.' Nor was he concerned with a merely normative impossibility. He did not want to say: 'I would very much like to do it, but unfortunately I cannot because it is forbidden.' No, Luther refused to act against his own conscience because, although it was factually possible and not forbidden, it would have been a most *unreasonable* thing to require of him. In the same way it is rationally impossible for someone who lives in the awareness of being favoured by God to reject this divine favour. In this sense the grace of God is 'irresistible' for a believer.

3.6 THE REFORMED DOCTRINE OF GRACE

In chapter 1 we argued that the task of Christian theology is to find a way of conceptualizing the Christian faith which is both coherent and adequate and at the same time does recognizable justice to the deeper intentions of the faith as it has been handed down to us in the religious tradition. One of the necessary conditions for fulfilling this task satisfactorily is that the systematic theologian should master an adequate philosophical or conceptual apparatus by means of which to express the required conceptualization of the faith. Without an adequate philosophical apparatus, the systematic theologian runs the risk of either achieving coherence but becoming untrue to the intentions of the tradition, or upholding the intentions of the tradition at the expense of coherence. In this way much systematic theology fails by becoming either incoherent or revisionary. This point is well illustrated by the attempt of the Synod of Dordt to produce an adequate conceptual expression for the Reformed doctrine of grace. The failure of the Reformed fathers at Dordt to produce a coherent conceptualization of their doctrine was due largely to the inadequate philosophical apparatus which they had at their disposal. In this chapter I have tried to show that using more adequate conceptual tools, especially with regard to the logic of personal concepts, relational concepts and modal concepts, can help us to give the Reformed doctrine of grace a more coherent formulation and at the same time do justice to the intention of this doctrine to maintain that salvation is by grace alone.[13] Let us conclude this chapter with some remarks about the role of these three kinds of concepts in the Reformed doctrine of grace.

[13] For other recent attempts at coherent conceptualization of the doctrine of grace in relation to human freedom, see David and Randall Basinger (eds.), *Predestination and Free Will* (Downers Grove, IL, 1968). See also George I. Mavrodes, 'Symposium: divine and human action', *Christian Scholar's Review*, 16 (1987), 384–404.

1 Personal concepts

There are two features which are of central importance in the
Reformed doctrine of grace which the Synod of Dordt tried to
express. No attempt at conceptualizing the Reformed faith can
be acceptable if it fails to do full justice to these. Firstly, this
doctrine is *theocentric* in nature. Salvation is a gift from God and
therefore all credit for it is due to him alone. *Soli Deo gloria!* As
human persons we have nothing about which we can boast.
'For it is by his grace you are saved, through trusting him; it is
not your own doing. It is God's gift, not a reward for work done.
There is nothing for anyone to boast of' (Ephesians 2:8–9). A
second important aspect of the Reformed doctrine of grace is the
fact that it speaks in *personal* terms about both God and human
creatures. It speaks about God as a merciful Father and about
us as persons who have rebelled against God and are responsible
for our actions in his sight. As we pointed out, the Canons of
Dordt (chapter 3/4, article 16) expressly state that not even the
Fall could take away the personal character of our humanity.

The problem now is how to do justice to both these aspects of
the Reformed doctrine without having them contradict each
other. In this chapter I have argued that this cannot be
achieved if we make use of causal models. The Dordt divines
tried to secure the theocentric character of salvation against any
threat of Pelagianism. As I have shown above, however, the
causal model that they used for this purpose has implications
which directly contradict the constituent presuppositions for
those personal concepts which they also use in what they claim
about our relationship with God. The Dordt divines were only
interested in forming a (radically negative) judgement on the
way in which we pervert our personal relation to God, but in
doing so they failed to pay attention to our personal nature as
such which remains intact in spite of sin. Indeed, we remain
persons, even when we turn our backs on God. In this chapter I
examined the conceptual implications of the claim that we are
and remain persons in relation to God. In doing so I made use
of a number of important observations about the implications of
personal concepts which Augustine (who certainly cannot be

accused of Pelagianism!) developed in his early anti-Pelagian treatise *De Spiritu et Littera*.[14]

In summary: Because the Reformed theologians at Dordt failed to pay attention to the constitutive presuppositions of the personal concepts which they used with reference to our relationship with God, it was not clear to them that these presuppositions contradict the causal model which they used in order to maintain the grace-given nature of salvation.

2 Relational concepts

It is not only a lack of insight into the necessary presuppositions of personal concepts that paved the way for the Dordt divines to use causal models. In my argument in this chapter I suggested that this could also be partly explained by the fact that they did not see human salvation in terms of a *personal relationship* with God, but in terms of a *reborn state* in us. States are brought about and thus ask for causal explanation. Personal relationships are entered into on a mutual basis and so ask for explanation in terms of the possibilities made available and the motives and reasons for realizing these possibilities. The fact that the theologians at Dordt had difficulty in formulating the issue in relational terms is not so surprising given the limitations of their philosophical apparatus. Let us explain.

Aristotle developed a logic of subjects and predicates: the subject term in a proposition is a name for a substance or thing and the predicate term is a name for an attribute or quality belonging to this substance. In the proposition 'Socrates is mortal', 'Socrates' is the name for a substance and 'mortal' is the name for an attribute or quality or state of this substance. This kind of logic generates an ontology where reality is seen as

[14] See especially chs. 53, 54, 58 and 60. In a recent paper, Ragnar Holte has shown that this doctrine of free choice is also defended in Augustine's early anti-Manichaean treatise on the freedom of the will and that he also maintained this view on free will after the Pelagian controversy. 'Certainly, the anti-Pelagian treatises represent, in many respects, further developments in Augustine's thinking, but *free will*, in its positive relation to *true freedom*, is in my opinion, conceived in *fundamentally* the same way both before and after the Pelagian controversy.' See Holte, 'St Augustine on free will', in '*De Libero Arbitrio*' *di Agostino D'Ippona* (Palermo, 1990), 84.

consisting of substances and attributes. The problem is that this leaves no room for relations given that a relation between substances is neither an attribute of one of these substances nor a third substance. If problems are formulated in terms of this sort of logic, the result is that relationships are inevitably reduced to qualities.

One of the many examples of this is the debate between Galileo and the ecclesiastical authorities on the question: Which of the two substances, the earth and the sun, is in a state of movement and which is in a state of rest? However, movement and rest are relations, not states: an object moves (or is at rest) only in relation to another object. The inadequacy of this form of the question becomes clear to anyone who has ever looked out of the window of a train at another train on the next platform at the moment when one of the trains begins moving, and then wonders which of the two is moving. This question only makes sense if the movement and rest of the trains is seen *in relation* to the station building and not in terms of the trains' relationship to each other – let alone as states in which the trains move or remain at rest irrespective of their relationship to other objects!

If, like the Dordt theologians, one does not have a more satisfactory philosophical apparatus than this kind of Aristotelian logic at one's disposal, it is clearly difficult to do otherwise than interpret salvation as a state caused in us by God. This does not provide an adequate account of the complex reciprocal nature of personal relationships in general, and of the personal relationship which we have with God in particular. In this chapter I have tried to develop Augustine's observations on personal freedom in a relational way in order to produce a philosophical apparatus with which more justice can be done to the claim that we have a personal relationship with God.

3 *Modal concepts*

It is not due only to insufficient insight into the logic of the personal and relational concepts that the theologians at Dordt fell back on a causal model in the formulation of their doctrine of grace. They also had positive reasons for doing this. As has

been shown above, these theologians were very deeply concerned with defending the theocentric character of salvation
against a theology of merit. In a causal model God is the one
and only cause of salvation, and to him alone all honour is due.
As human beings we have no grounds for pride or self-
satisfaction.

In this chapter I have tried on the one hand to show that a
bad tool is being used here for a good purpose. The use of a
causal model implies that it is factually (or causally) impossible
to resist the grace of God, and this is in direct contradiction to
the constituent conditions for a personal relationship between
us and God. On the other hand, by means of an analysis of the
modal concepts 'possible' and 'impossible', I have suggested an
alternative solution in which salvation is seen as participation in
a personal relationship with God (existing in the love of God).
Here it is not factually impossible for the believer to resist grace,
but certainly impossible in the sense of being unreasonable. The
question is now whether this alternative is a viable one. Is
sufficient justice done here to the theocentric nature of
salvation?

If salvation consists in having a personal relationship of
mutual love with God, then there are three necessary and
jointly sufficient conditions for salvation. Firstly, we must be
persons, given that only persons can participate in a personal
relationship. That we are persons is due only to the fact that
God has made us persons. He could have made us into 'senseless
stocks and blocks', but in his omnipotent love he chose not to do
that. To him be all honour and glory! Secondly, the fact that we
are persons before God does not yet imply that we are able to
enter into a relationship with God, and thus achieve our own
salvation. Even if we wanted to, we *could not* achieve this unless
God made it possible for us by offering us his love. By definition
we can neither compel nor oblige God to offer us his love. For
this condition for salvation we are therefore also dependent on
the omnipotent grace of God. To him be all honour and glory!
The third necessary condition for achieving this relationship
with God is that we have to choose to enter into it. Reformed
theology is very conscious of the fact that in our sinful state we

are neither aware that God loves us nor inclined to respond to his love. On this account we are also unable to provide the third necessary condition for our salvation. This can only be achieved if God reveals his love to us in Christ and inspires us by his Spirit to respond to it. God must himself convince us of the only valid *reasons* to respond to his love, namely the fact that he loved us first and revealed his love for us in Christ. It is the love of Christ that 'constrains' us (2 Corinthians 5:14). In this way the third necessary condition for our salvation is also provided by God. To him be all honour and glory!

On reaching this point the temptation is great to fall back on the causal model and to interpret this 'constraint' as the causal bringing about of a *state* in us rather than as the inspiring motivation by which we are enabled to make a *choice*. *Causal manipulation* makes things factually inevitable for us and thus eliminates our making any choice at all. In this way the first of the above-mentioned necessary conditions for salvation (as participation in a personal relationship with God) is overriden. *Motivating inspiration*, on the other hand, confronts us with a choice and is therefore by definition never factually irresistible. In this sense it remains *factually* possible for someone who is constrained by the love of Christ, still to turn his back on God. From the point of view of faith, this would be the most highly unreasonable thing that a human person can do, since it would be contrary to the most powerful reason by which our actions could ever be motivated, namely the fact that God loved us first.

Does this view do justice to the Reformed claim that salvation is by grace alone? Are we required to do something (i.e. choose to love God) for which we can claim any credit? Can we boast of the fact that we received the incomparable *favour* of being loved by God and have chosen to do that for which God himself has provided us with the strongest reasons imaginable, namely to respond to his love? These questions should only be asked in order to show how absurd they are from the point of view of faith!

In brief: With respect to all the necessary conditions for our salvation, honour and glory is due to God alone. His love is the only and overriding reason for us to love him. *Soli Deo gloria!*

Having claimed this, however, the believer is faced with a further immense problem. If turning our backs on God is rationally impossible in this very strong sense, why then do we do it? And why does God not prevent us from doing it? In brief, why is there evil in the world? We will return to this question in chapter 6.

CHAPTER 4

Can God do evil?

4.1 'IMPECCABILITAS'

In the previous chapter we argued that the possibility of entering into a personal relation with God is a fundamental presupposition of both the Christian life and the Christian faith. This entails that both God and human beings are persons and therefore free agents who are able to take the initiative with regard to their own actions in relation to each other. We argued that one consequence of this presupposition is that human beings have the ability to do evil by resisting the grace of God. We now have to deal with the question whether the same holds for God as the other partner in the relation. If God is a free agent, is he also free and able to do evil? Would that not contradict another fundamental presupposition of Christian faith and life, namely that God is perfectly good?[1]

In the Christian tradition God's perfect goodness has generally been held to entail that he has the attribute not only of *impeccantia* (freedom from sin), but also of *impeccabilitas* (inability to sin). Thus, for example Aquinas held that 'God is unable to will anything evil. Hence it is evident that God cannot sin';[2] and according to the Westminster Confession, 'God… being holy and righteous, neither is nor can be the author or

---

[1] In a recent article, Robert F. Brown has argued that God need not be perfectly good but that he needs to be morally vastly superior to any other being. This opens up the possibility of God willing evil and performing evil actions. See Robert F. Brown, 'God's ability to will moral evil', *Faithful and Philosophy*, 8 (1991), 3–20. In this chapter I hope to show that there is no need for so radical a revision of the traditional doctrines of divine goodness and impeccability.

[2] *Summa contra Gentiles*, III.25.

approver of sin'.[3] Although there is general agreement on the claim that it is impossible for God to sin, there is no such agreement about the sense in which this is impossible. Because of the notorious ambiguity of modal terms like 'possible', 'impossible' and 'necessary', the doctrine of divine impeccability is open to various interpretations.[4] Let us inquire how it could best be interpreted coherently within the context of Christian faith.

We shall start with some preliminary remarks about the terms 'sin' and 'God'. If we were to define 'sin' as 'alienation from God', it can only be applied in a straightforward sense to creatures and not to God himself. It would therefore be uninformative to claim that God cannot sin in this sense. Adapting the phrase quoted above from the Westminster Confession, we could argue, however, that the doctrine of divine impeccability denies that God can sin in the sense of 'being the author or approver of evil'. Four remarks need to be added here. 1. We shall interpret 'being the author of *p*' in a broad sense to include 'bring about *p*', 'command that *p* should be brought about' as well as 'permit that *p* should be brought about'. 2. We shall also interpret 'evil' in a broad sense to include sin (as the alienation of human persons from God), moral wrongdoing and suffering. 3. In order to allow for God's permitting forms of evil which are in some way or other entailed by some higher good, we shall furthermore interpret 'evil' to mean 'evil for its own sake'. In other words, although God never *intends* evil to occur, he does not prevent those forms of evil which are *unintended* consequences, concomitant effects or side effects of the realization of his (good) intentions. We shall return to this point in section 5.4 below. On this definition the doctrine of divine impeccability excludes both that God be the author and that he be the approver of evil. In other words, if God

---

[3] *Westminster Confession*, ch. v, sect. iv.

[4] For some recent interpretations, see for example Bruce R. Reichenbach, 'Why is God good?', *Journal of Religion*, 60 (1980), 51–66 (see also his *Evil and a Good God*, New York, 1982, ch. 7); Thomas V. Morris, *Anselmian Explorations* (Notre Dame, IN, 1986), 42–69; Thomas F. Tracy, 'The moral perfections of God', *The Thomist*, 47 (1983), 473–500; Ingolf U. Dalferth, 'Gott und Sünde', *Neue Zeitschrift für systematische Theologie und Religionsphilosophie*, 33 (1991), 1–22.

cannot sin then (a) he cannot *approve* of evil, and (b) he cannot be the *author* of any state of affairs of which he does not approve. (We shall argue that these are both impossible, but not in the same sense.)

With regard to the term 'God' we shall follow Nelson Pike in interpreting it as a special type of descriptive expression, that is, what he calls a 'title term'.[5] To affirm of an individual that he is God is to affirm that that individual occupies a special position or has a special value status in relation to everything else. We could describe this position and status with the phrase used by St Anselm: God is a being than which nothing greater can be conceived (*aliquid quo majus nihil cogitari potest*). Part of what is meant by ascribing this status to an individual is to claim that the will of that individual counts as the ultimate standard of all goodness. The affirmation that x is God therefore entails the affirmation that the will of x is the ultimate standard of all goodness: whatever x approves of is to count as good, and whatever x disapproves of is to count as evil.

While 'God' is to be construed as a title term, 'Yahweh' is the name of the individual who, according to the Judaeo-Christian tradition, is the bearer of this title. It is therefore definitive of being a Christian that one should consider Yahweh to be a being than which nothing greater can be conceived and hence also that Yahweh's will is the ultimate standard of all goodness.

4.2 CONCEPTUAL IMPOSSIBILITY

Equipped with these distinctions, let us now inquire into the sense of 'impossible' involved in the doctrine of divine impeccability. We assumed above that two things are impossible according to this doctrine: that God should be the author of any state of affairs of which he does not approve, and that God should approve of any state of affairs which is evil.

With reference to the first of these it is clear that (in the terminology introduced in section 3.2 above) there is nothing

---

[5] Nelson Pike, 'Omnipotence and God's ability to sin', in P. Helm (ed.), *Divine Commands and Morality* (Oxford, 1981), 68. See also Nelson Pike, *God and Timelessness* (London, 1970), ch. 2.

conceptually impossible (or impossible by definition) about somebody being the author of a state of affairs of which he or she does not approve. Human nature being what it is, it happens all too often that we do things of which we disapprove! If, however, we take the term 'God' to be a title term in the sense explained, then it is conceptually impossible *for God* to be the author of anything of which he does not approve, even though this is the sort of thing human beings often do. After all, doing what one does not approve of is a sign of weakness and not of perfection, and since 'God' means 'a being than which nothing greater or more perfect can be conceived', it would be conceptually impossible for an individual to be God and to exhibit this form of human weakness.

If we also take approving evil to be a sign of imperfection, then it is similarly conceptually impossible for an individual to be God and to approve of evil. Here, however, we have to do with a second, even stronger form of conceptual impossibility as well. We assumed that if an individual is God, then that individual's will counts as the ultimate standard of goodness. This entails that whenever such an individual should approve of something, it cannot count as being evil, for his approving of it is what ultimately determines that it is good and not evil. We could also explain the difference between these two forms of conceptual impossibility by comparing the following two propositions which are both analytic, but for different reasons: 1. 'if *x* is God, *x does not* do anything which *x* does not approve' and 2. 'if *x* is God, *x conceptually cannot* approve of evil (since whatever *x* approves, conceptually cannot count as evil)'. The first is analytic because part of the definition of an individual being God is that that individual only does what he approves. The second is analytic because part of the definition of an individual being God is that that individual's will is the ultimate standard of goodness.

If we substitute 'Yahweh' for 'God' in these two propositions, they are, however, not analytic. The propositions 'Yahweh does not share the (human) imperfection of doing things he does not approve' and 'Yahweh's will is the ultimate standard of goodness' are in themselves not conceptually necessary. They are only conceptually necessary (*de dicto*) *relative to a particular context*, that is, the context of the affirmation that Yahweh is God. This affirmation is not analytic. There are many who deny it and they do not commit a *logical* or *conceptual* mistake by doing so. They do however commit what believers claim to be a *religious* mistake because what they deny is a fundamental affirmation definitive for the Christian faith. In the light of this analysis, it is conceptually necessary *within the context of the Christian faith* to affirm that Yahweh is God and hence also that 1. Yahweh is in fact never the author of any state of affairs of which he does not approve, and 2. Yahweh's will being the ultimate standard of goodness, it is conceptually impossible for him to approve what is evil. It is only possible to deny these two propositions if we also deny that Yahweh is God and in this way reject the Christian faith as such.

Although these two propositions seem on the one hand to be necessary within the context of the Christian faith, they seem on the other hand to be either inadequate or to have some uncomfortable implications for the believer. As to the first proposition, one could ask whether believers do not want to claim more than that Yahweh in fact *never does* anything of which he does not approve. Would believers not also want to claim that in some sense it is *impossible* for Yahweh to do so? And in what sense of 'impossible' would they want to claim this? (We shall return to these questions in section 4.6 below.)

The second proposition seems to conflict with at least three other affirmations implied in the believer's claim that Yahweh is God. First of all, if Yahweh is God, then he is omnipotent. Does this not conflict with the proposition that it is conceptually impossible for him to approve of evil? Secondly, if Yahweh is God, then he is a rational agent in the sense of having reasons for what he does or approves. He cannot approve of something for no reason whatsoever, for that would make his approval irrational or capricious. If, however, his approval is the ultimate standard of goodness, he cannot be said to approve of anything *because* it is good since it is by virtue of his approval that it counts as being good. In other words, if his approval is the ultimate standard of goodness there can be no further standard which could be appealed to as a reason for his approval. In the third place, if Yahweh is God, then he is perfectly good. But as Nelson Pike points out, 'in so far as the phrase "perfectly good" applies to the individual that is God (Yahweh) as an expression of praise – warranted by the fact that this individual does not sin – God could not be perfectly good if he does not have the ability to sin'.[6] If it is conceptually impossible for Yahweh to approve of evil, then he cannot be praised for not doing so.

Let us first deal with the three objections against the proposition that if Yahweh is God, it is conceptually impossible for him to approve of evil. The first objection is the easiest to answer. If by 'omnipotent' we mean 'having the creative power to bring about any coherently describable state of affairs',[7] then Yahweh's omnipotence is in no way contradicted by the claim that it is conceptually impossible for him to approve of evil. It remains conceptually possible for him to *approve* of any coherently describable state of affairs. All that is conceptually excluded is that whatever he does in fact approve of could be counted as being evil. Whether he is also able to *bring about* a state of affairs of which he does not approve, and whether it would contradict his omnipotence if he could not, is another matter with which we shall deal in section 4.6 below. So much for the first objection. In order to deal with the other two we must first examine what it means to claim that Yahweh's will is the *ultimate standard* of goodness.

[6] Pike, 'Omnipotence and God's ability to sin', 80. This point was also raised by Leibniz in par. 11 of his *Discourse on Metaphysics*. Cf. Anthony Flew, *An Introduction to Western Philosophy* (London, 1971), 28–9. That the ability to sin is required for God's moral praiseworthiness is denied by Edward Wierenga, *The Nature of God* (Ithaca, NY, 1989), 212–13.

[7] Cf. Pike, 'Omnipotence and God's ability to sin', 69, for an argument that Aquinas' definition of omnipotence should be interpreted in this way.

4.3 ABSOLUTE AND RELATIVE VALUES

It is important here that we distinguish clearly between absolute and relative values.[8] The relative value of something is the value it has in relation to some purpose or standard. Thus the chair on which I am now sitting is good relative to a purpose, that is, it is good for sitting on while writing at a desk, but not for relaxing in (for that a lounge chair would be better), or for sitting on at a bar (for that a bar stool is better). My desk is a metre long relative to my tape measure. My tape measure (which is old and probably no longer quite accurate) is a metre long relative to the more accurate measuring rod at the physics laboratory. This measuring rod is a metre long relative to the so-called 'standard metre', that is, the distance between two scratches on a platinum-iridium bar kept in the archives in Paris. Absolute values differ from relative values in not being the values things have in relation to a purpose or standard, but the value of some *ultimate* purpose or standard. As these are ultimate, their value by definition cannot be relative to some further purpose or standard. The proposition 'the scratches on the Paris bar are one metre apart' is therefore not a judgement relative to some further standard (as is the proposition 'my desk is one metre long'); it is rather an affirmation that this counts as the ultimate standard in the light of which we determine whether or not anything else is a metre long. The value of my ultimate aim in life is also not determined in relation to some further aim: it *is* the ultimate aim.

An important implication of these differences between absolute and relative values is that doubt about the one is very different from doubt about the other. Doubting whether my desk is one metre long is doubting whether it has the same length as the distance between the scratches on the Paris bar. Doubting whether the distance between the scratches on the Paris bar is one metre is absurd.

Although we cannot doubt whether the standard metre is one

[8] Cf. D. Z. Phillips, *Faith and Philosophical Enquiry* (London, 1970), 798ff, and Patterson Brown, 'God and the good', *Religious Studies*, 2 (1967), 269–76.

metre long, we can meaningfully doubt whether we should accept the Paris bar as ultimate standard for our system of measurement. This, however, is a very different sort of doubt. It cannot be formulated or settled *within* the framework of the metric system of measurement. It is a doubt about the acceptability of the metric system as such. This sort of doubt cannot be settled in the light of any criteria *interior* to the metric system but only in the light of practical criteria *exterior* to the system and applied to the system as such.

The history of the metric standard is instructive with regard to this point. The French National Assembly decided in 1791 to introduce the metric system of measurement. They then defined the metre to be 'one ten-millionth part of a meridional quadrant of the earth'. It took two French scientists six years to determine how long that is. Obviously a standard of measurement which is so difficult to determine is not very convenient. Imagine having to take six years to check the accuracy of my measuring rod! In order to avoid this difficulty, they constructed a standard metre bar in accordance with the results of their measurements of the earth, and presented this to the National Assembly in 1799. Thus a metre was then defined in terms of the length of the standard metre bar. Most Frenchmen, however, found it more convenient to go on using the old familiar system of measurement, and it was not until 1840 that the French government managed to get the metric system enforced all over France. During this century the standard metre bar has proved to be too imprecise a standard for use in scientific measurements. For this reason the metre has been redefined a number of times, most recently at the 17th General Conference on Weights and Measures where the metre was defined as 'the distance which light travels in a vacuum in one 299792458th of a second'. This standard is not only more precise but also more readily available since it can be reproduced anywhere and not only in Paris where the standard metre bar is kept.

In brief, although it is conceptually impossible to judge the ultimate standard of a system of measurement in terms of the criteria *internal* to the system, it is possible to judge this ultimate standard along with the system of measurement as such in terms of *external* standards such as precision, availability, constancy, applicability, and so on, and so decide whether or not to adopt the system and its ultimate standard as such.

4.4 YAHWEH'S WILL AS ULTIMATE STANDARD

We argued above that, within the Christian faith, the will of Yahweh is affirmed to be the ultimate standard of goodness. Yahweh's will is absolutely good, and not good relative to some more ultimate standard of goodness. Hence the judgement 'what Yahweh approves of is good' is not a judgement on Yahweh in the light of some higher standard of goodness, but an affirmation that his will is the ultimate standard. *Within* the Christian faith there is no more ultimate standard of goodness.

Although there are no further internal standards within the Christian faith by which to judge the ultimate standard of goodness, there are some external standards which anything has to fulfil if it is to function as a standard of goodness at all.[9] Thus, for example, it should at least be available, universally applicable and consistent. Let us examine these three criteria.

First of all, we saw that defining the metre in terms of the measurements of the earth proved unsatisfactory because the ultimate standard arrived at in this way was not easily available. It is for anybody far too time consuming and difficult to produce. Similarly, Yahweh's will could hardly be an ultimate standard of goodness if it were impossible for anybody to know what Yahweh does or does not approve. In spite of the difficulties involved in deciding what Yahweh's will is in *every* situation in which we have to act, Christians have always claimed that Yahweh does reveal his will sufficiently to believers to enable them to appeal to it as ultimate standard of goodness.

Secondly, all standards should be universally applicable in order to be used as standards at all. If situations should arise in which a standard cannot be applied by anybody, then it ceases to be useful as a standard. Thus, for example, the standard metre bar has proved inapplicable in modern scientific measure-

---

[9] On the distinction between internal and external standards, see my *Theology and Philosophical Inquiry* (London, 1981), ch. 10.

ment, being too imprecise for anybody to measure millionths of a millimetre with it. For this reason it has in fact been discarded as ultimate standard and replaced by the much more precise standard defined in terms of the distance light travels in a split second. Similarly, if a situation should arise where it is in some way impossible for someone to accept Yahweh's priorities, then it becomes existentially impossible for that person to apply Yahweh's will as ultimate standard of goodness. D. Z. Phillips gives a good example to illustrate this point:

One might have heard someone talk of what it means to accept a tragedy as the will of God. He might have explained what Jesus meant when he said that a man must be prepared to leave his father and mother for his sake by pointing out that this does not imply that children should forsake their parents. What Jesus was trying to show, he might say, is that for the believer the death of a loved one must not make life meaningless. If it did, he would have given the loved one a place in his life which should only be given to God. The believer must be able to leave his father and mother – that is, face parting with them – and still be able to find the meaning of his life in God. Listening to this exposition, one might have thought it expressed what one's own beliefs amounted to. But then, suddenly, one has to face the death of one's child, and one realizes that one cannot put into practice, or find any strength or comfort in, the beliefs one has said were one's own. The untimely death of one's child renders talk of God's love meaningless for one. One might want to believe, but one simply cannot.[10]

Someone in this situation understands what it would mean to maintain the priorities approved by Yahweh as ultimate standard of goodness, but he is so overcome by affliction that he is existentially unable to maintain them in fact.

This sort of problem is not a problem *within* the Faith (believers know how it should be solved within the Faith), but a problem *about* the Faith. Whether or not a specific believer is able to maintain his faith in the face of affliction depends very much upon the strength of that believer's faith, and therefore provides no indication whether Yahweh's will is somehow inherently inapplicable for everyone as ultimate standard of goodness. Not everyone faced by affliction would follow Ivan

---

[10] Phillips, *Faith and Philosophical Enquiry*, 99–100.

Karamazov and rebel against Yahweh and his priorities. Some might even conclude with Simone Weil that it is only when we suffer affliction that we are able to learn what the love of Yahweh really means.[11] From this it is clear that the will of Yahweh can only count as ultimate standard of goodness if believers are in fact able (at least with Yahweh's help) to apply this in their own lives. There are enough examples of believers who not only affirm this possibility but also realize it in their lives – even in the face of affliction.

Another external standard which something has to meet in order to function as a standard at all is consistency. It is for this reason that the standard metre bar was made of platinum-iridium which is not influenced by temperature changes. If it had been made of mercury like a thermometer, it would have become longer or shorter with every slight change in temperature in Paris and thus become useless as a standard of measurement. Using such a standard would have the absurd consequence that all things are continually changing in size according to the temperature changes in Paris! Similarly, if Yahweh were to be capricious, continually changing his mind, approving of something one moment and disapproving of it the next, then his approval could not function as an ultimate standard of goodness. Christians affirm, however, that Yahweh's will is unchanging: he remains consistent in what he approves and disapproves and in this way faithful to his own nature or character. It is clear that for this reason Plato could not consider the will of the (Greek) Gods as an ultimate standard of value. His Gods were not only capricious, but they all willed different things. Hence Plato had to introduce eternal moral truths to which the will of the Gods was to be subjected. In the Euthyphro he therefore had Socrates defend the position that the Gods should approve of actions because they are good (i.e. in accordance with the eternal moral standards) rather than that actions are good when they are in accordance with the will of the Gods. In the Christian tradition, theologians like

[11] Simone Weil, 'The love of God and affliction', in Weil, *On Science, Necessity and the Love of God* (London, 1968). See also Eric O. Springsted, *Simone Weil and the Suffering of Love* (Cambridge, MA, 1986), 39–52.

Augustine and Anselm interpreted the platonic ideas as ideas in the mind of God and Plato's eternal moral truths as identical with the will of Yahweh. This entails a different position on the Euthyphro dilemma from that defended by Socrates: There are for the believer no eternal moral truths by which to judge the will of Yahweh, since the will of Yahweh is the ultimate standard of goodness.[12]

We can conclude that believers do not only accept Yahweh's will as ultimate standard of goodness, but also claim that it in fact fulfils the external criteria (availability, applicability and consistency) which make it suitable to be such an ultimate standard.

In the light of this analysis we can now answer the two remaining objections raised above against the view that Yahweh's will is the ultimate standard of goodness, namely that it implies that Yahweh cannot be a rational agent (since he could have no reasons for approving of anything) nor praiseworthy for not approving of evil (since it is conceptually impossible for him to do so). Yahweh's will is rational, not because it always conforms to some standard of goodness external to it, but because it remains consistent to itself. Yahweh remains faithful to his own character in what he approves and disapproves. Similarly, although Yahweh cannot be praised for remaining faithful to some standard of goodness external to himself, he can be praised for remaining faithful to himself and not acting out of character.[13]

4.5 THEOLOGICAL NECESSITY

From our argument thus far we can now draw the following conclusions regarding the nature of divine impeccability:

(A) It is analytically true that *God cannot sin*, in the sense that it

---

[12] For a similar view on the Euthyphro dilemma, see Richard Swinburne, *Responsibility and Atonement* (Oxford, 1989), 126.

[13] This eliminates the dilemma raised by Robert Brown, that an ontologically good God cannot at the same time be morally good, without having to resort to the radically revisionary solution which he proposes. See Brown, 'God's ability to will moral evil', 15ff.

would be contradictory to claim of any individual that he is both God and also the author and approver of evil. This is so because part of what it means to claim that *x* is God is to claim the following:

1 *x*'s will is the ultimate standard of goodness (which implies that *x* cannot be the *approver* of evil);
2 *x* in fact never acts out of character by:
   (a) bringing about what he does not approve of (and thus being the *author* of evil), or
   (b) failing to fulfil the necessary conditions under which his will could count for us as the ultimate standard of goodness, by
      (i) not making his will adequately known to us, or
      (ii) willing that we live up to standards of goodness which are in fact impossible to realize, even with divine help, or
      (iii) being capricious or inconsistent in what he wills.

(B) It is not analytically true in this sense that *Yahweh cannot sin*. It may be false (as believers claim) to assert that Yahweh is the author and approver of evil, but not contradictory. There is, however, another sense in which it is impossible to assert that Yahweh is the author and approver of evil. J. J. C. Smart explains this with an example from physics.[14] According to Smart it is not conceptually necessary that light should have a constant velocity in a vacuum. We could deny this without contradiction. Yet this proposition is so fundamental to all current physical theory that we cannot deny it without rejecting or at least radically revising all current physical theory. *Within current physical theory* this proposition cannot be denied. That Yahweh is not the author and approver of evil is also not conceptually necessary. Nevertheless, this affirmation is definitive for the Christian faith, and cannot be denied without rejecting the Christian faith as such. *Within the context of the*

[14] J. J. C. Smart, 'The existence of God', in A. Flew and A. MacIntyre (eds.), *New Essays in Philosophical Theology* (London, 1955), 40.

Christian faith this affirmation cannot be denied. In this sense it is what we could call *theologically necessary*.

4.6 'DE DICTO' AND 'DE RE'

Even if we accept the conclusions reached so far, it is doubtful whether they are adequate as an account of what is claimed in the doctrine that Yahweh is impeccable. The same doubts arise here which we expressed in section 4.2.

The trouble is that 'theological impossibility' is merely a form of impossibility *de dicto*, concernings what *cannot be said* within the context of the Christian faith, and not impossibility *de re* about what *cannot occur* in reality. This becomes clear if we compare the following two questions: 1. Can Yahweh act out of character (by bringing about what he does not approve, or by failing to fulfil the conditions necessary for his will to count as ultimate standard of goodness)? 2. Can a believer affirm that Yahweh does act out of character, without thereby abandoning the Christian faith as such? To say that it is 'theologically impossible' for Yahweh to act out of character is to answer the second question negatively, whereas the doctrine of impeccability gives a negative answer to the first. Furthermore, if we state the second question in this way, it merely deals with the believer's claim of *impeccantia* (that Yahweh in fact does not act out of character) and not with that of *impeccabilitas* (that it is somehow impossible that he should do so) as well. We have, therefore, to extend our analysis to include impeccability *de re*. This could be done by dealing with the following two questions: 1. Is it theologically necessary to claim not only that Yahweh does not act out of character, but also that it is somehow impossible *de re* for him to do so? 2. If this were the case, what sort of impossibility would be required?

We could answer the first question by showing that the claim that Yahweh is God entails the further claim that he not only does not but also *cannot* act out of character. In affirming that Yahweh is God, believers base the meaning of their lives on their faith that Yahweh will remain true to his promises and will not deviate from his character. If, however, it is a purely fortuitous contingency that Yahweh remains true in this sense, believers would hardly have sufficient warrant to base so much on their faith. As St Augustine puts it,[15] if we love a perishable object, we live in constant fear of losing it and this is incompatible with true happiness. True happiness is only possible when we put our trust in someone eternal who does not merely *happen* not to change, but who is in some sense immutable and unable to change. In some sense, therefore, it is necessary within the context of the Christian faith to claim that Yahweh *cannot* deviate from his character. In what sense of 'cannot' is it necessary to claim this?

Even though persons in fact often act out of character, some would claim it is *conceptually impossible* for Yahweh to do so. Unlike the character of a human person, Yahweh's character has to be interpreted as an *essential nature* which logically necessitates his acting in accordance with it. According to Richard Swinburne, who defends this sort of view, God 'is so constituted that he always does what there is overriding reason to do, and always refrains from doing what there is overriding reason for not doing. He always does what is good because that is how he is made.'[16] Leaving aside the difficulties involved in this kind of essentialism, as well as the question whether logical necessity can in this way be construed as a form of necessity *de re* and not merely as a form of necessity *de dicto*, this view raises some other formidable problems. If Yahweh is effectively prevented from acting out of character by the way he is 'constituted' or 'because that is how he is made', then the fact that he stays faithful to his character is not a matter of choice but of lack of creative power. He would then be more like an infallibly 'constituted' machine, only able to behave in accordance with the way it is made, than like a person freely deciding what to do or not to do. Thus the three difficulties raised in section 4.2 above appear again, and this time they cannot be satisfactorily answered. Yahweh could hardly be called omnipotent in the sense of having the creative power to

[15] Augustine, *De Moribus Ecclesiae Catholicae*, ch. 3. See also Etienne Gilson, *The Christian Philosophy of Saint Augustine* (London, 1961), 4.
[16] Richard Swinburne, *The Coherence of Theism* (Oxford, 1977), 182.

bring about any coherently describable state of affairs. Neither could he be considered to be a rational agent: his character would not provide a *reason* for his acting the way he does. It would be a logically sufficient *cause* effectively making it impossible for him to act in any other way. In fact, what Swinburne calls 'overriding reasons' cannot be reasons at all, but have become necessitating causes. Furthermore, if Yahweh is in this way powerless to deviate from his character, he could hardly be praised for not doing so.

Nelson Pike suggests a sense in which one could claim that Yahweh cannot act out of character, without at the same time denying that he has the creative power to do so. According to Pike, Yahweh's character is such that it provides us with 'material assurance' that he will remain faithful to it:

This is the sense in which one might say that Jones, having been reared to regard animals as sensitive and precious friends, just *cannot* be cruel to animals. Here 'cannot' is not to be analyzed in terms of the notion of logical impossibility, and it does not mark a limitation on Jones's physical power (he may be physically able to kick the kitten). It is used to express the idea that Jones is *strongly disposed* to be kind to animals.[17]

Although Pike avoids the objections we raised against Swinburne, it is by no means certain that his view provides for a sufficiently strong 'material assurance' against Yahweh's acting out of character. After all, no matter how strongly a human person like Jones may be disposed against being cruel to animals, situations could very well arise in which he nevertheless acts contrary to his disposition. If Yahweh's disposition against acting out of character is not materially different from that of a human person, it could hardly provide an assurance strong enough to justify the believer's basing the meaning of his life on it. Perhaps we could adapt Swinburne's argument in such a way that it provides for such a material difference without limiting Yahweh's creative power or his freedom of choice.

There are two ways in which we could explain the fact that people act out of character by doing things against which they have overriding reasons and thus would be strongly disposed

[17] Pike, 'Omnipotence and God's ability to sin', 81.

not to do. They could on the one hand do so through ignorance of the situation. Thus, for example, Jones could have kicked the kitten because he mistook it for a ball of wool. On the other hand, although people are sometimes not mistaken about the facts of the situation, they nevertheless fail to do what they know they should because they are prevented from doing so by some physical or psychological constraint. Thus, Jones could have been so angry at the kitten for eating the goldfish that he could not help himself kicking it.

Swinburne argues that Yahweh differs from all human persons in being both *omniscient* and *perfectly free* from all constraints which could prevent him from acting in accordance with his character.[18] Hence none of the reasons which explain human weakness of will apply in the case of Yahweh. Whereas human persons could be strongly disposed not to act out of character, Yahweh, being omniscient and perfectly free from constraint, is what we might call 'divinely disposed' not to do so. This fact about Yahweh provides believers with material assurance against Yahweh acting out of character such as they can never have in the case of any human person.

Unfortunately, Swinburne goes further than this, and interprets the divine disposition as something which logically necessitates Yahweh to act the way he does. He argues that 'it is logically necessary that an omniscient and perfectly free being... will always do an action if he judges that there are overriding reasons for doing it rather than for refraining from doing it'.[19] In this Swinburne goes even further than what he himself calls 'the extreme position' of R. M. Hare, 'that necessarily if a man judges that A is the better action, he will do A unless it is psychologically impossible for him to do A'.[20] On the one hand, this kind of view ignores the fact that even though irrational action is incoherent and therefore inexplicable, it is nevertheless possible in fact. In terms of our argument in section 3.5 above, the rational impossibility of an action does not entail

[18] Swinburne, *The Coherence of Theism*, ch. 8.   [19] Ibid., 182.
[20] Ibid., 148. For Hare's view see his *Freedom and Reason* (London, 1963), ch. 5. For criticism of Hare, see G. W. Mortimore (ed.), *Weakness of Will* (London, 1971), especially the contributions of Steven Lukes and Irving Thalberg.

its factual impossibility. On the other hand, as we have shown, this view also mistakenly interprets overriding reasons as sufficient causes.

We can now conclude as follows: For believers who claim that Yahweh is God, it is theologically necessary to affirm (*de dicto*) that Yahweh cannot sin (*de re*) in the sense that he is divinely disposed in this way. Believers are therefore warranted to base the meaning of their lives and their eternal happiness on the faithfulness of Yahweh, their God.

CHAPTER 5

Can God act in the things we do?

5.1 DOUBLE AGENCY: FARRER AND WILES

In section 2.5 we argued that using the conceptual model of personal relations in thinking about our relationship with God entails the claim that both God and human beings are personal agents in relation to each other, and therefore both free in the sense of being able to take the initiative with regard to their own actions in relation to each other. In chapters 3 and 4 we discussed two problems that arise from these claims about human and divine freedom respectively. In this chapter we will examine the nature of the relation between divine and human agency within such a personal relationship. If both God and ourselves are personal agents in relation to each other, how are divine and human agency related?

A central tenet of Christian belief is the claim that God acts in the world in a variety of ways in order to realize his purposes. Christian believers usually also hold that this divine agency is in principle indirect: God is always a primary cause acting by means of secondary causes and never intervening directly on the level of the secondary causes.[1] Thus we can never 'treat God as just one more causal agent among others in the world'.[2] In this

---

[1] It is sometimes argued that God might circumvent secondary causes by performing 'basic acts'. See on this, for example, William P. Alston, *Divine Nature and Human Language* (Ithaca, NY, 1989), 85, 197. See also Thomas F. Tracy, *God, Action and Embodiment* (Grand Rapids, MI, 1984), 82ff.

[2] Maurice Wiles, *God's Action in the World* (London, 1986), 56. See also Austin Farrer's warning against thinking of divine agency in a way in which 'we degrade it to the creaturely level and place it in the field of interacting causalities. The result can only be…monstrosity and confusion.' Farrer, *Faith and Speculation* (London, 1967), 62.

way divine agency is claimed to take effect in and through the natural order and also through the acts which human agents perform. In this chapter we will limit ourselves to the latter kind of 'double agency' (i.e. that involving the acts of human agents), since this is especially relevant for our inquiry into the relation between divine and human agency. Thus, according to Austin Farrer, 'we may say of the Hebrews, that they commonly saw divine effects as having creaturely agents'.³ Similarly John Burnaby claims that 'the power of God's love takes effect in human history in no other way than through the wills and actions of men in whom that love has come to dwell'.⁴ The claim that God acts 'through the wills and actions of men' raises a number of conceptual difficulties which seem so intractable as to cast doubt on the intelligibility of the concept of divine agency as such.⁵

The key issue here has to do with interpreting what Farrer calls the 'causal joint' between divine and human agency in such a way that it does not deny the personal integrity of human agents 'through the wills and actions' of whom God is said to act. Since this problem is basic to Austin Farrer's theory of 'double agency' as well as to Maurice Wiles's work on divine agency, their views will serve in this chapter as point of departure in the light of which we could discuss the nature of double agency. I will on the one hand try to show that neither of them is able to provide a satisfactory solution to this problem, and on the other hand I will suggest an alternative interpretation of the claim that God is the agent of our actions, which is both coherent and does full justice to our integrity as personal agents.

---

³ Ibid., 62. For an extensive discussion of Farrer's theory of double agency, see B. L. Hebblethwaite and E. Henderson (eds.), *Divine Action* (Edinburgh, 1990).

⁴ John Burnaby, 'Christian prayer', in A. R. Vidler (ed.), *Soundings* (Cambridge, 1962), 232–3.

⁵ 'The problems posed by the questions "Does God act in the world? And if so, in what ways, and by what means?", are of such magnitude that it seems highly probable that some significant shift away from traditional answers to those questions may be called for.' Wiles, *God's Action in the World*, 13. Wiles also considers the comparable difficulties which are raised by the claim that God acts in and through the natural order. I have discussed these at some length in chapter 5 of my *What Are We Doing When We Pray?* (London, 1984).

As we point out above, Austin Farrer considers the concept of double agency to be characteristic of the way in which divine agency is described in the Bible. On this point Maurice Wiles concurs.[6] However, both of them are also very much aware of the conceptual difficulties involved in this view. In what sense can we claim that God acts 'through the wills and actions of men' without thereby denying their personal integrity as agents? If God were to bring about our actions, do we not thereby cease to be the personal agents of these actions and become rather the impersonal tools used by God to exercise *his* agency? If on the other hand human persons were to remain the originators of their own actions (as they must if these are to be ascribed to them), how can these actions then also be ascribed to God as though they were *his*? In brief, does it make sense to ascribe the same action to two different agents? Thus Farrer admits that 'two agents for the same act would be indeed impossible, were they both agents in the same sense and on the same level...If God were a voluntary agent just as I am a voluntary agent, my good deed could not be his work, for it is mine.'[7] Farrer tries to get out of this difficulty by means of 'that mossy piece of scholastic lore, "analogical predication"'[8] in terms of which he concludes that 'it is true that I am unequipped to think of God's agency otherwise than in terms of my own; it is false that I believe it to be of the same sort'.[9] Unfortunately he fails to provide any positive indication of what sort it *is* and therefore ends in agnosticism concerning the causal relation or 'causal joint' between divine and human agency. 'Both the divine and the human actions remain real and therefore free in the union between them; not knowing the modality of the divine action we cannot pose the problem of their mutual relation.'[10] Farrer tries to mitigate this admission of ignorance

---

[6] 'Farrer regards the concept of double agency – that is seeing happenings in the world as acts of both God and man – as a fundamental feature of the biblical record and of Christian experience. On the first score, its role in the biblical story, the issue seems to me beyond dispute.' Wiles, 'Farrer's concept of double agency', *Theology*, 84 (1981), 244.   [7] *Faith and Speculation*, 104.   [8] Ibid., 104.
[9] Ibid., 104–5. The tenuous nature of this analogy becomes clear when Farrer states on page 23 that the causality of divine action 'can be no more than distantly analogous to any finite causality productive of a finite effect'.   [10] Ibid., 66.

by claiming that anyway knowledge of the nature of this causal joint is irrelevant to religious belief. 'The causal joint (could there be said to be one) between God's action and ours is of no concern in the activity of religion; the very idea of it arises simply as a byproduct of the analogical imagination ... Surely it is nothing new that imagination should fall over its own feet, or symbolism tangle into knots.'[11] Clearly then, since Farrer fails to provide an explanation of the way in which divine and human agency are related, the nature of double agency remains mysterious. 'In the end the understanding of divine agency offered is so distantly analogical and so unrelated to the causal story that we tell of the happening of events, that we appear to be left without even a direction in which to look to give intelligibility to the concept of particular divine actions of the kind that he affirms.'[12] In spite of his dissatisfaction with Farrer's account, Wiles shares Farrer's agnosticism with regard to the 'causal joint' between divine and human agency and concludes that it might be better to dispense with the concept of double agency altogether.[13] Instead he proposes a kind of deism: 'Such a view is not deistic in the most strongly pejorative sense, in that it allows for a continuing relationship of God to the world as source of existence and giver of purpose to the whole. It is deistic in so far as it refrains from claiming any effective causation on the part of God in relation to particular occurrences.'[14] The key term here is 'particular'. Wiles's point is that the doctrine of creation entails God's granting of freedom and autonomy to created reality in general and to human persons in particular. Every claim that a *particular* event or human action is to count as an act of God would, however, be a denial of this

---

[11] Ibid., 66. Wiles comments as follows on this move: 'I am unhappy with this emphasis. It is a bit like the answer to the question "what was God doing before he made heaven and earth" which Augustine reports but repudiates: "He was preparing hell for those who pry too deep".' Wiles, 'Farrer's concept of double agency', 247.   [12] Ibid., 348.

[13] 'We do not understand the modality of divine action in a way which enables us to define its relation to our finite human acting. But this fact makes me chary of speaking in terms of "double agency" with the confidence that Farrer does.' Wiles, 'Farrer's concept of double agency', 248.

[14] Wiles, *The Remaking of Christian Doctrine* (London, 1974), 38.

freedom and autonomy.[15] Hence Wiles proposes that 'the primary usage for the idea of divine action should be in relation to the world as a whole rather than to particular occurrences within it...The whole process of the bringing into being of the world, which is still going on, needs to be seen as one action of God.'[16] But how are these particular occurrences and human actions related to this one comprehensive divine action? According to Wiles this relation is to be understood as that between a number of subacts and one master-act:

A complex action of this kind necessarily contains within itself a number of secondary actions, which together help to make up the one complex act...But...a master-act may be made up of subacts whose agent or agents are other than the agent of the master-act. Solomon's building of the temple necessarily involved many subacts, but he does not himself have to be the agent of any of them in a sense distinguishable from his being the agent of the master-act.[17]

Unlike Gordon D. Kaufman, to whom he is indebted for this distinction between master-act and subacts, Wiles refuses to speak of 'God performing any of the subacts which together contribute to God's one act of creating our world'.[18] It is clear that Wiles denies here any form of causal relation between God's master-act and the particular acts performed by human agents. In this way, however, the claim that the latter can count as 'subacts' of the former becomes quite vacuous and the relation between divine and human action becomes no clearer than with Farrer: since Farrer remains agnostic about the 'causal joint', the relation between divine and human action remains a mystery. Since Wiles denies any form of 'causal joint', the relation becomes vacuous.

On the other hand, the position with Wiles might be less bleak than it appears at first sight. His Bampton Lectures contain a number of clues which might be developed into a more satisfactory view on double agency. But then these clues

---

[15] At this point Wiles parts company with Farrer who holds that 'if God acts in this world, he acts particularly; and if I had no conception of the particular lines along which his purpose works...I could not associate my action with the divine and the whole scheme of religion as we have set it out falls to the ground.' *Faith and Speculation*, 61.   [16] Wiles, *God's Action in the World*, 28–9.   [17] Ibid., 96.

[18] Ibid., 97. For Kaufman's views, see his *God the Problem* (Cambridge, 1972), 119–47.

have to be integrated into a more satisfactory view on causality than that which both Farrer and Wiles seem to presuppose.

5.2 THE CAUSAL JOINT

According to the doctrine of double agency, God realizes his purposes in the world through the actions of human agents. If by this is meant that God realizes his purposes by *causing* us to act according to his will, then it would seem that God is the only agent involved. We are in no way the originators of the action as we should be if we were to count as its agents. Similarly, if Solomon built the temple by *causing* the labourers to lay one stone upon another, then he rather than they becomes the agent of these acts of bricklaying. The labourers become merely the tools by means of which Solomon exercises his agency. We have seen how Farrer responds to this by affirming the reality of both the divine and the human action and pleading ignorance about the causal joint between them. This merely ignores the problem and does not solve it. Wiles tries to deal with the problem in terms of the distinction between God's master-act and our subacts. By denying that God is in any way the agent of our subacts, however, the causal joint between the master-act and the subacts is denied and the relation between divine and human agency becomes no clearer than in the case of Farrer.

As we suggested above, the source of confusion here is the concept of causality in terms of which the problem is conceived, namely the idea of a causal chain in which each link is the sufficient antecedent condition for the next link. If indeed God's action is the sufficient antecedent condition for what I do, then there is no room for agency on my part. However, this conception of causality is far too simple. For every event, the complete set of antecedent conditions which are together sufficient to bring the event about consists of an infinite number of conditions, all of which are necessary, but not one of which is sufficient by itself. This is also true when the event in question is an action performed by a personal agent.

As we argued in section 3.3, I am as an agent the originator of my own actions in the sense that my free choice to perform them is a *necessary* condition for their occurrence. In this way what I *do* differs from what *happens* to me regardless of what I choose.[19] However, my choice is never a *sufficient* condition for my own action. I cannot perform an action merely by choosing to do so. Unless my factual circumstances are such as to enable me to do what I choose to do, I cannot perform the action. As we argued in section 3.3 above, my freedom to act is always a concrete freedom: I am only free to realize the possibilities given in my concrete situation, and not to do just anything what-soever. The *sufficient* condition for an action being performed therefore consists of the conjunction of the agent's choice and the complete set of factual circumstances which make it possible for the agent to perform the action in question.

Since the choice to act must of logical necessity be made by the agent himself, nobody can bring about the sufficient conditions for the action of someone else. In this sense one person cannot bring about the act of another. However, one person can always bring about some of the necessary conditions for the action, other than the choice made by the agent. You could provide me with the means without which I could not perform the action, or the motive without which I will not perform it. But the means and the motive are not sufficient to bring about the action unless I choose to perform it. Thus one person's action can be a *contributory* cause, but not a sufficient cause of the action of someone else. In this way it is possible to overcome Farrer's agnosticism about the 'causal joint' between divine and human agency and explain in what sense God can realize his will through the 'actions of human agents, who freely intend to further the purposes of God, seek God's grace to enable them to do so, and do in fact achieve their intended

---

[19] Clearly, what is required for something to count as an action is freedom in the sense of *choice* and not merely in the sense of *consent*. I can also consent to things that happen to me regardless of my decision, and these would not count as actions of mine. The traditional (rather confusing) terms for these two concepts of freedom are the 'liberty of spontaneity' and the 'liberty of indifference'. For a useful discussion of this distinction, see chapter 7 of Anthony Kenny, *Will, Freedom and Power* (Oxford, 1975), and chapter 2 of Kenny's *Freewill and Responsibility* (London, 1978). Kenny correctly argues that both these concepts refer to necessary conditions for an adequate concept of moral freedom. It is therefore wrong to view them as alternative complete concepts of freedom, as is often done.

goal'.[20] He cannot do this by *causing* their choices, for then they would cease to be the agents of these actions. But he can make his will known to them, as well as enable and motivate them to do what he wills. In this way God provides the *conditiones sine quibus non* for the human agents to realize his will, without thereby denying their freedom and integrity as agents. On the contrary, it is still up to the human agent to do God's will, and if he chooses not to (in spite of knowing God's will and being enabled and motivated to do it), then God's will is not done. In this way double agency is a matter of co-operation between two agents and not of one agent using the other as a tool.

5.3 ASCRIBING ACTIONS TO GOD

So far so good. Even Wiles admits that in these ways God can provide the necessary conditions for our doing his will.[21] But is this sufficient reason for *ascribing* such acts to God? Wiles doubts whether it is: 'Even in such cases the problems concerning divine grace and human freedom make it uncertain whether and in what sense one can appropriately speak of them as God's acts.'[22] J. R. Lucas[23] develops an important distinction which could help us out here. He points out that we normally talk about 'the cause of an event' in two ways. Sometimes we use this expression to mean the *complete* cause of the event, that is, the complete set of causal conditions which together are sufficient to bring about the event. There are two aspects of this set of causal conditions which are especially important within the present context. First of all, to be logically complete, the set

---

[20] Wiles, *God's Action in the World*, 98. Farrer's agnosticism makes him claim that the believer 'does not and cannot relate [his conduct] to any supposed point at which an underlying act of the divine power initiates or bears upon creaturely action' (*Faith and Speculation*, 105).

[21] In his *God's Action in the World* Wiles explicitly affirms the role of God's revealing, enabling and motivating activity in this connection. Thus he affirms that (a) God provides us with some awareness of his intention (p. 102) and makes possible human recognition of his intention (p. 103); (b) God enables us to act (pp. 18, 34), bestows on us the capacities for action (p. 20) and makes our response to his intention possible (p. 103); (c) God wins the hearts and minds of people to work for the desired end (p. 22), acts like a friend who stands by me and encourages me to make my own choice (p. 99), and takes initiatives which are persuasive but not coercive (p. 78).

[22] Wiles, *God's Action in the World*, 98.

[23] J. R. Lucas, *Freedom and Grace* (London, 1976), ch. 1.

of necessary causal conditions would have to include negative conditions (the electric lights will only go on if the technicians are *not* on strike at the power station) as well as standing conditions (the match will only ignite if there is oxygen in the earth's atmosphere). Although we often ignore these conditions or take them for granted when giving causal explanations, they are nevertheless an essential part of the complete cause. Secondly, in the case of actions, the complete cause necessarily includes the decision of the agent, and can consequently never be brought about by somebody else.

However, we use the expression in another way as well. We select one of the causal conditions included in the complete cause and call that *the* cause in the sense of the most important or most significant factor in bringing about the effect. The considerations in the light of which we select the most significant factor are complex, and different considerations are relevant in different circumstances. Thus for example we sometimes ask for *the* cause of an event from curiosity as to why it occurred at that specific time and place and in that specific way. In that case *the* cause will be the factor which is most peculiar to the effect and not those factors like the negative and standing conditions which would also apply if the effect were to take on another form or occur at another time and place. Thus *the* cause of the match igniting now is my striking it rather than the oxygen in the atmosphere, and *the* cause of the first world war would be the shot fired at Sarajevo rather than Prussian imperialist ambitions which would probably have led to a war anyway but in conjunction with other factors at another time and in another way. Or else we select *the* cause from the point of view of the manipulator who wants to know what to do in order to bring about an effect. In that case we choose the factor which is within our power to bring about and we ignore the standing conditions which we can take for granted. If we want to light the fire, we strike a match and take it for granted that there is oxygen in the atmosphere.

When the event in question is an action, we usually select as most important the causal factor which we hold responsible, or to which we ascribe praise or blame for what has been done.

Sometimes we select the agent's decision as the most important factor and therefore hold the agent responsible for the effect, but this is not necessarily the case. We could also hold one of the other factors responsible (including the negative or standing conditions) or even the action of another agent in bringing one or more of these factors about. Thus for example,

The coroner will say the cause of death was drowning, the unsuccessful rescuer will think the cause was his failure to dive well enough, the teenage chum will know that it was his folly in having dared his friend to swim to the wreck, the mother that it was having let him go out swimming on such a nasty cold day, the father that it was his having failed to instil more sense and more moral courage into his head.[24]

As we argued in section 3.6 above, believers will in this way always say *soli Deo gloria!* and give God the credit for their own conversion or spiritual successes: if it were not for the fact that God revealed his will to me and enabled me and inspired me to do it, I would never have done it. Therefore, to him be all praise and thanksgiving! In thus considering God as 'the cause' of his own action, the believer does not, of course, deny that he performed it himself and of his own free will!

Believing in human freedom, as a Christian must, he cannot refuse to speak in the first person. I did it: I could have done otherwise, but I chose to do it. But as soon as he has said this, he has said too much, arrogating to himself a credit that is God's, and speaking as though he were of himself sufficient to obtain his own salvation: so he goes on to say at once 'Yet not I, but God in me', and attributes all to the grace of God rather than himself, meaning by the grace of God all those factors which he recognizes as having been at work in his own conversion and pilgrimage, apart from himself.[25]

Lucas also points out that we often not only give one person the credit for what was performed by another, but we even speak of the one as having 'done' what strictly speaking was carried out by others. Thus 'we speak of Solomon's having built the temple, though it is doubtful whether with his own hands he so much as placed one stone upon another. Thus our ordinary way of speaking allows us to talk not only of one person's having caused the actions of another, but of his having done them.'[26]

---

[24] Ibid., 4.   [25] Ibid., 13.   [26] Ibid., 7.

Clearly, then, there is nothing incoherent in ascribing to God responsibility for our actions (and even in talking of God as 'doing' our actions), without thereby having to deny our own freedom and personal integrity as agents. Interpreted in this way, the concept of double agency can even account coherently for those cases which seem especially puzzling to both Farrer and Wiles, namely 'actions by human agents, who have no conscious intention to further any believed purpose of God, but who do in fact achieve results that Christians believe to be of great significance for the furtherance of that divine purpose'.[27] Of course in such cases we cannot claim that God reveals his intentions to the agents in question, since they are unaware of his intentions. Nor can we claim that God inspires them to realize his intentions, for their intentions are other than his. But we can say that God realizes his intentions by enabling them to do, or at least not preventing them from doing, what they intend. Since God's non-prevention is a *conditio sine qua non* for their action, it is quite coherent to hold God responsible for bringing about the effects of their action.

5.4 IDENTIFYING DIVINE ACTIONS

So far so good. At one point even Wiles seems to suggest that in some such way we can meaningfully thank God (and thus presumably ascribe responsibility to God) for the effects of what human agents do.[28] However, this solution raises some serious

---

[27] Wiles, *God's Action in the World*, 98 (see also pp. 60–3). In such cases, according to Wiles, 'there does not seem to be any intelligible way of relating the intention of God and the human deed performed, which would be a necessary condition for describing it as a specific action of God' (p. 98). According to Farrer 'Isaiah was convinced that the Assyrian invasions were the scourge of God, a Father's correction of his sons' rebellion. But he knew that the Assyrians were not somnambulists under a divine hypnotism. The Assyrian was a rod in the hand of God's indignation, but he had no notion of being anything of the kind. His motives were acquisitive or political' (*Faith and Speculation*, 61). Farrer has great difficulty in seeing how the prophet could suppose that such divine influence could come to bear on the Assyrians, and concludes that 'such an idea is impossible to us in anything but poetry' (p. 62).

[28] 'Human speech fulfils many roles and the appropriate style of speech varies accordingly. "It's all thanks to you! It's all your doing!", I may say to a friend who has stood by me and encouraged me to make my own choice. That is a proper use of language in the context of the expression of gratitude' (*God's Action in the World*, 99;

difficulties, since it seems to prove more than we bargained for. In the case of finite agents, the range of events which they can bring about, or the occurrence of which they are able to prevent, is very limited indeed. It is therefore relatively simple to identify those events for which a finite agent might be held responsible as distinct from those which are beyond his or her control. Since God is omnipotent, however, nothing is beyond his control and no event could ever take place without his agency being involved.

No theist would deny that God is omnipotent, and that he could intervene to prevent any particular event's occurring, and that therefore his non-intervention is a necessary condition of each event...Rome fell, we say, because God did not intervene to save it. But if Rome had not fallen, we should equally ascribe that to God's non-intervention, in the same way as we do ascribe its survival in previous centuries to God's forbearance. That is, whether Rome falls or not, God is the cause.[29]

This raises two serious difficulties. First of all, the claim that God brings about *all* events excludes the possibility of identifying particular events as acts of God as distinct from the rest which we ascribe to other agents. This entails that we should hold God responsible for all events, both good and evil, including all actions performed by human agents. Secondly, the claim that all events are brought about by God would seem in the end to make all talk of divine agency vacuous. Is there not 'something vacuous in adding *Deo volente* to every prediction and every causal statement, because if it is to be *said* always, we could equally well *understand* it always, leaving it unsaid'?[30]

As we explained above, Wiles tries to avoid difficulties like these by means of his distinction between master-act and subacts: God is the agent of the one master-act which includes 'the whole process of the bringing into being of the world',

see also his argument on pp. 74–5). However, Wiles seems to think that in some way this use of language is merely figurative and not 'intended to be understood in a directly descriptive way'. In fact, 'it would be misleading if taken literally as a straightforward account of the genesis of my action'. Maybe in the end Wiles proceeds no further than Farrer's conclusion which we quoted in the previous footnote: 'Such an idea is impossible to us in anything but poetry.'
[29] Lucas, *Freedom and Grace*, 9.   [30] Ibid., 9.

whereas all *particular* events and actions both good and bad within the created world are ascribed to finite agents and not to God. In this way the problem of having to identify which particular events are to be ascribed to God does not arise for Wiles. I have difficulty in making sense of this proposal as it stands: it is incoherent to claim that God is the agent of everything *and* of nothing in particular, and it is vacuous to claim that God's action has no particular content.

It may be that the concept of causality which we developed in the previous section might help us out with these problems. Three points are important here.[31] Firstly, if God can intervene to prevent any particular event occurring, no event is possible unless God allows it to occur. Divine agency is therefore part of the complete cause of *every* event, and in this sense his agency is not finite like that of human persons. Secondly, if the concept of double agency is taken to mean that God acts *only* through secondary causes, then God never lets his own agency be the complete cause of any event. His agency is one of the necessary conditions for every event, but not the only one, since he has decided to allow for secondary causes to co-operate with him in what he does. These secondary causes are independent originators of action with whom God has decided to share his power. This independence is of course *relative* and not absolute, since it is bestowed on the secondary causes by God who is able at any time to take back what he has given. As we have argued in section 3.6 above, the very fact that we are personal agents rather than 'stocks and blocks' is also due to the grace of God. It is due to God's grace that we do not exist in a deterministic universe in which divine agency is the complete cause of all events. Such a universe would be contrary to God's aim in creating an orderly context in which human persons can exist and freely co-operate with him in the realization of his purposes, a context in which personal fellowship is possible between God and human persons. If this is the sort of universe God wants to bring about, he *logically* cannot do so if his agency is the complete cause of every event. Thirdly, if for every event divine

---

[31] For a more extended development of these ideas, see my *What Are We Doing When We Pray?*, ch. 6.3. See also ch. 5.

agency is one but not the only necessary causal factor, then divine agency need not necessarily be the factor held responsible for every event. Since we praise him for the occurrence of some events, he is held responsible for their occurrence. But this does not exclude our ascribing responsibility for other events to other factors necessary for their occurrence. From the fact that God could have but did not prevent Auschwitz, it does not necessarily follow that we must hold him responsible for Auschwitz.[32] We could instead hold Hitler and his henchmen responsible, as in fact we usually do.

The problem of identifying particular divine actions now becomes a problem of deciding when we are to hold divine agency responsible for an event and when we are to lay the responsibility elsewhere instead. The conceptual problem here depends on the nature of the ascription of responsibility in personal relations. Let us look at the way we decide this in the case of human agents. There are various considerations which play a role in this sort of decision. First of all, we do not hold someone responsible for an event unless his or her agency is one of the necessary conditions for its occurrence. Thus we do not praise or blame someone for an event which he or she could not have prevented because it was beyond his or her control. This consideration limits the range of events which can be ascribed to any particular finite agent, since most events are beyond the control of such an agent. However, this consideration does not help us in distinguishing God's actions from those events which cannot be ascribed to him, since as we have argued, his agency is infinite in the sense that it is a necessary condition for every event. Secondly, even when a human agent could have prevented an event, we do not hold him or her responsible if he or she could not have foreseen the event in question. Thus we do not blame someone for unforeseeable effects of his or her actions. If the agent could have foreseen the effect but failed to do so

---

[32] Here I differ from Nelson Pike, 'Over-power and God's responsibility for sin', in A. J. Freddoso (ed.), *The Existence and Nature of God* (Notre Dame, IN, 1983), 29–33, as well as from William E. Mann, 'God's freedom, human freedom and God's responsibility for sin', in T. V. Morris (ed.), *Divine and Human Action* (Ithaca, NY, 1988), 182–210. Mann offers a rather deterministic account of double agency.

because he or she did not bother to find out, we could blame him or her for *negligence*, that is, 'voluntary unawareness of the nature of one's action'.[33] If the agent foresaw the likelihood of the effect, but did not care whether it occurred or did not bother to count the cost of its occurring, we could blame him or her for *recklessness*.[34] Obviously neither of these considerations is relevant in the case of God, for in his omniscience God can foresee all future possibilities and probabilities.[35] Also God is never negligent or reckless in what he does because he knows the cost without first having to count it, and can therefore never be blamed for failing to count it or find it out.

There is however a third consideration which applies even when somebody *knows* that his agency is a necessary condition for an event and that he is therefore able to prevent its occurrence. This is whether his action is *intended* to bring about the event in question. What do we mean by calling an action *intentional*? According to Anthony Kenny 'an agent intends an action if (a) he knows he is doing it and (b) does it because he wants to do it for its own sake or in order to further some other end'.[36] Kenny distinguishes such intentional actions from their foreseen consequences, concomitant effects and side effects. These are not intentional because bringing them about is not part of the reason for performing the action. The agent is of course able to avoid bringing them about, but only at the price of giving up the purposes or chosen means of which they are unintended consequences or side effects.[37] Thus, although the agent does not *want* these in the strict sense of intending them, he does want them in a minimal sense of *consenting* to their occurrence.

To say that an agent wants to do X, in this minimal sense, is merely to say that he does X consciously while knowing that it is in his power to refrain from doing X if only he will give up one of his purposes or

---

[33] Kenny, *Freewill and Responsibility*, 6.   [34] Ibid., 63.

[35] Not all future actualities! This entails a limit to divine foreknowledge. See chapter 3 of my *What Are We Doing When We Pray?* See also Wiles, *God's Action in the World*, 63.

[36] Kenny, *Will, Freedom and Power*, 56. See also Kenny, *The Metaphysics of Mind* (Oxford, 1989), 38–9, 45.   [37] Kenny, *Will, Freedom and Power*, 57–9.

chosen means. The wanting in question is mere willingness or consent: it is quite different from any feeling of desire, and may be accompanied with varying degrees of enthusiasm diminishing to reluctance and nausea.[38]

These distinctions are important in determining whether we are to hold an agent responsible when he knows that his agency is a necessary condition for the occurrence of an event, or whether we should rather hold responsible some other factor also necessary for the event to occur. We only ascribe direct responsibility to someone for what he does intentionally and not for unintended consequences or side effects of his actions. In cases where the event in question is not the effect which your action is intended to achieve, but some unintended consequence or side effect of your action, then I may only hold you responsible for letting the achievement of your purpose prevail above avoiding the unintended consequence or side effect of your action. Here, too, I am in fact holding you responsible for the purposes which you *intentionally* try to realize or allow to prevail in your action. In all cases, therefore, where your action is a necessary condition for an event occurring, whether I ascribe the bringing about of the event to you depends on the *intention* with which you did what you did. Thus the English common law maxim *actus non facit reum nisi mens sit rea* (an act does not make someone guilty unless his mind is guilty too)[39] applies in general to the ascription of responsibility to agents.

In brief: ascription of responsibility applies only to *actions* and not merely to observable *behaviour*. Since any adequate description of an action must include a reference to the intention with which the agent behaved the way he was seen to behave, we cannot simply equate someone's action with his observable behaviour. It follows that I can only ascribe the effects of your observed behaviour to you if I know what your intention was in behaving in the way you did. The problem is that I cannot infer this knowledge merely from what I perceive you to have done.

---

[38] Kenny, *Freewill and Responsibility*, 51. See also Kenny, *The Metaphysics of Mind*, 45–6.
[39] For an interesting discussion on the principle of *mens rea*, see Kenny, *Freewill and Responsibility*, chs. 1 and 3.

I have rather to interpret what I perceive you doing in the light of my *prior knowledge* of your intentions.[40] But how do I get to know what you intend? There are three main ways in which I can know your intentions. First of all, I can know what you intend because you tell me. Secondly, I can infer your intentions from my knowledge of your character. Thus I presume that you are not acting out of character and that your intentions now are the same as I knew them to be when you were acting in similar circumstances in the past. Thirdly, I can infer your intentions from my knowledge of human nature or of the moral standards of the cultural community to which you belong. I presume that your intentions in doing what I perceive you to do are similar to those I know myself and other people (especially those belonging to the same culturally community as you do) to have when they act under similar circumstances. Thus in deciding whether to ascribe an event to you when your agency is a necessary condition for its occurrence, I have to *interpret* the occurrence in the light of what I believe to be your intentions.

This analysis of intentional action also applies when we decide whether we are to ascribe an event to God. Even though God's agency is a necessary condition for every event, this does not entail that we should identify every particular event as an act of God. We only ascribe those events to him which he brings about *intentionally* and not those events which are unintended side effects of his intentional acts. In other words, we only ascribe those events to his agency in which he realizes his purposes, and not events which he permits even though they are contrary to his positive will. 'There is much that is contrary to God's positive will. He may permit, but he does not countenance or condone. Angels and men are in open rebellion against him.'[41] This analysis enables us on the one hand to agree with Wiles that 'the whole process of the bringing into being of the world, which is still going on, needs to be seen as one action of God',[42] on condition that we take this to mean that God's

[40] On this point, see Charles M. Wood, 'The events in which God acts', *The Heythrop Journal*, 22 (1981), 278–84.
[41] P. R. Baelz, *Prayer and Providence* (New York, 1968), 81.
[42] Wiles, *God's Action in the World*, 29.

agency is a necessary condition for the occurrence of every event which takes place in the world. Contrary to Wiles, we can on the other hand also make sense of the claim that some particular events rather than others may be identified as acts of God, in the sense that we hold God's agency responsible for them and not for the others, even though he could have prevented these others from occurring.

5.5 THE EYE OF FAITH

As in the case of finite agents, we cannot infer God's intentions from the events which we perceive to happen, but rather decide whether or not these events are to be interpreted as divine acts, in the light of our prior knowledge of God's intentions.[43] But how do we acquire this knowledge? Above we noted three ways in which we get to know the intentions of finite agents: from what they tell us, from our knowledge of their character, and from our knowledge of the intentions of other people when acting in similar situations. The last of these does not apply in the case of God, since he is unique: his intentions and purposes are not analogous to those of other people, and cannot therefore be arrived at by analogy to those of other people. 'My thoughts are not your thoughts, and your ways are not my ways. This is the very word of the Lord' (Isaiah 55:8). Also the first of these ways does not apply to God in the way it does to other people. You could inform me about your intentions in performing any specific act, but what would it be like for God to inform me about his intentions with any specific event which he causes or allows? If I should have an experience which I take to be God telling me his intentions, how do I know that this is really God speaking and not merely my own imagination? If I should have such an experience (similar to those of the prophets in the Bible), I would have to test it in the light of the tradition of faith, which comprises the cumulative experience of the community of

---

[43] In this sense Wiles's attempt to 'tread the path of inference' (ibid., 57) is misguided and bound to fail, since the events which we perceive to happen in the world can never of themselves provide the 'unmistakable evidence of particular acts of God' (ibid., 74) which Wiles seems to require.

believers through the ages.[44] But then our knowledge of God's intentions is more like the second of the three ways in which we know the intentions of other people; we infer God's intentions regarding specific events from our cumulative knowledge of his character and purposes.

In this way the tradition of faith provides the believer with an interpretative framework in the light of which to decide whether to identify specific events as particular intentional acts of God. In this sense I can agree with Farrer that 'a Christian has his accepted works of the divine hand, which give him his types of Providence in action. In view of these he appreciates the ever-new works of God.'[45] Whether any event is to be interpreted as a divine providential action is like the doctrine of providence as such in that it 'cannot simply be read off empirical fact. It is an interpretation of fact in conjunction with a prior belief in the Creator.'[46] But then, considering an event as an act of God is not a matter of perception, but of interpretation with the 'eye of faith'.[47] This also applies to all those events which we take to be acts of God in which he enables or inspires us to do his will, or in which he reveals his will to us. It is only with the eye of faith that we can interpret an event, a sermon, a book, and so on as a revelation of God.[48] If we were to interpret Wiles along these lines, then he is correct in emphasizing the *retrospective* character[49] of all talk about divine agency: we cannot predict precisely

---

[44] For an elaboration of this point with special emphasis on the role of the biblical narrative, see Ronald F. Thiemann, *Revelation and Theology: The Gospel as Narrated Promise* (Notre Dame, IN, 1985), 108ff. Thiemann argues that the notion of double agency is intelligible 'provided there are available procedures for identifying and distinguishing the acts and intentions of the two agents' (pp. 106ff).

[45] *Faith and Speculation*, 64.

[46] B. L. Hebblethwaite, 'Austin Farrer's concept of divine providence', *Theology*, 73 (1970), 543. In this way the claim that a particular event is an act of God is not a straightforward empirical claim which can be subject to some sort of empirical test.

[47] This is correctly emphasized by Diogenes Allen, 'Faith and the recognition of God's activity', in Hebblethwaite and Henderson (eds.), *Divine Action*, 197–210.

[48] In this way the claim that God can be known from his works seems to entail an infinite regress (see Wiles, *God's Action in the World*, 57). Elsewhere I have tried to show how this regress might be avoided. See my *Theology and Philosophical Inquiry* (London, 1981), 270–5.

[49] Wiles, *God's Action in the World*, 64, 81, 89. Compare also Farrer's remark that 'God's agency does not strike us in the springing-point of causes but in the finished effect' (*Faith and Speculation*, 63).

what God will do at any particular moment in the future. We can however retrospectively interpret particular events as acts of God because of the way they fit into the general pattern of what we take to be God's intentions. It is interesting to compare this with Aristotle's point about the events in a good story: they always occur unexpectedly, but in retrospect their occurrence is recognizably reasonable since it can be seen to arise out of the structure of the plot.[50]

Our ability to recognize God's actions by looking at the world through the eye of faith is never infallible. Believers all too readily tend to identify their own preferences with the will of God and consequently ascribe events to God because they fit in with these preferences. Recognizing God's actions in the world requires training in the religious practice of conforming our preferences and prejudices to the pattern of God's intentions. In this sense we can agree with Farrer's remark that 'the question, how we make out or identify the line of the divine action, is a question of detail, of practice, and of day-to-day religion'.[51] In this practice prayer has an important part to play: 'When praying, the believer is...repeatedly making himself see the world in a certain way in which everyday experiences are fitted into what he thinks is the proper reality; he is repeatedly bending his emotional life and his behaviour to conform to this reality.'[52] In this way prayer becomes what John Drury calls 'the school of seeing'.[53]

By our thus interpreting experience of the world in terms of God's gracious agency, the world acquires religious meaning for the believer:

God sends the rain to the just and the unjust: but to the just who has asked for it, it comes as a token of God's goodness, whereas to the unjust who never says 'please' and never says 'thank you', it is a mere climatic condition, without significance and without being an occasion for gratitude; and the unjust's life is thereby poorer and drearier.[54]

---

[50] Aristotle, *Poetics*, 1452a.   [51] Farrer, *Faith and Speculation*, 61.
[52] A. Alhonsaari, *Prayer: An Analysis of Theological Terminology* (Helsinki, 1973), 47–8.
[53] J. Drury, *Angels and Dirt: An Enquiry into Theology and Prayer* (London, 1972), ch. 1.
[54] Lucas, *Freedom and Grace*, 38.

CHAPTER 6

Can a theodicy console?

6.1 CONSOLATION AND MORAL SENSITIVITY

In chapter 4 we came to the conclusion that an almighty and perfectly good God will always remain faithful to his own character and can therefore be counted on never to become the author or approver of evil. This conclusion immediately confronts us with the classical problem of evil, which was also raised at the end of chapter 3: If God is not the author or approver of evil, why then do we encounter so much evil and suffering in the world? Cannot an omnipotent God prevent all evil and suffering from ever occurring in the world, if in his goodness evil and suffering are abhorrent to him? In the previous chapter we argued that God is not the author or approver of evil in the sense that evil and suffering are contrary to his intentions and therefore never brought about by him intentionally. However, this does not prevent God's consenting to forms of evil and suffering which are *unintended* consequences, concomitant effects and side effects of the realization of his intentions in the world. But what are these greater goods intended by God which have such evil side effects? In the Christian tradition this perennial problem has usually been answered by some or other form of theodicy argument and especially by the so-called *free will defence*.[1] In section 2.5 we pointed out that the free will defence is based on our thinking of

---

[1] For recent expositions and defences of this argument, see for example Stephen T. Davis, *Logic and the Nature of God* (Grand Rapids, MI, 1987), 97–117; Michael L. Peterson, *Evil and the Christian God* (Grand Rapids, MI, 1982); Bruce Reichenbach, *Evil and a Good God* (New York, 1982), ch. 7.

God in terms of personal models: if God intends to create us as persons who can enter into a personal relationship with him, he must accept the risk that we should abuse our freedom as persons and cause evil and suffering in the world. It follows that if we were to reject the free will defence, and hold with Ivan Karamazov that a good God should not accept this risk, then we will also have to take leave of such personal models when thinking of God and our relationship to him.

It should be noted that the free will defence is primarily intended to account for moral evil, that is, the evil and suffering which result from the abuse of human freedom and responsibility. It does not account for physical evil, that is, suffering caused by natural catastrophes and diseases which do not result from the abuse of human freedom. We shall point out below that the exercise of human freedom and responsibility does require a world in which physical suffering is *possible*, but this is not sufficient to explain the *actuality* of physical suffering in the world. However, the point we made in the previous chapter does apply to both moral and physical evil. All forms of evil and suffering are contrary to the divine intentions, and are therefore only permitted by God as the unintended consequences of the realization of his intentions. It follows that the occurrence of all physical evil which is in no way connected with the abuse of human freedom, should be understood as the unintended consequence of the realization of divine intentions other than the establishment of personal relations with us. We will, however, limit our discussion here to the implications of the free will defence and not speculate about what these further divine intentions might be,[2] since that would divert us from the aim of these chapters, which is to explore the implications of using personal models for thinking of our relationship with God. For this purpose, it is more important to discuss a significant practical objection to all such attempts at reconciling human suffering with the love of God: arguments like the free will defence usually fail to offer any consolation to the afflicted. On the contrary, such theodicy arguments are often experienced as

---

[2] I have dealt with this issue elsewhere, See my paper 'Het kwaad en de goedheid van God', *Nederlands Theologisch Tijdschrift*, 36 (1982), 29–51.

morally insensitive by those who suffer. Arguments which try to show that their suffering is in accordance with the goodness and the love of God fail to take their suffering seriously. In section 2.5 we noted how such considerations caused Ivan Karamazov to rebel against God. In this light we might question whether believers are ever justified in using arguments like the free will defence if they prove to be morally insensitive and therefore fail to offer consolation to the afflicted. Is Helen Oppenheimer not right in doubting whether believers have 'any right to assure miserable people that their sufferings are somehow taken care of in God's whole scheme of things'?[3] In fact, do arguments like the free will defence not conflict with the claim that God is a God of love: if God is really a God of love, would it not be incoherent to attribute the moral insensitivity of such arguments to him? On the other hand, however, we have shown that the free will defence is based on the presupposition that God is a personal being with whom we might maintain a personal relation. Does rejecting the free will defence entail that we should reject this presupposition as well? Or can the apparent moral insensitivity of the free will defence be explained in the light of the insensitive way in which it is usually stated and defended? Is it not possible to state and defend the free will defence in such a way that it loses its moral insensitivity and succeeds in consoling the afflicted?

As a point of departure for dealing with these issues in this chapter, I would like to discuss the debate between Richard Swinburne and D. Z. Phillips about the problem of evil.[4] After

---

[3] Helen Oppenheimer, *The Hope of Happiness* (London, 1983), 171. See also Isabel Wollaston, 'Starting all over again', *Theology*, 93 (1990), 456–62, who argues that only the individual sufferer can interpret his or her fate, and that we should listen to the victims of suffering rather than construct theodicies.

[4] This debate consists of a paper by Swinburne, a critical response by Phillips, some remarks by John Hick and postscripts by both Swinburne and Phillips. These papers were published in Stuart C. Brown (ed.), *Reason and Religion* (Ithaca, NY, 1977). More recently Swinburne restated his arguments in *The Existence of God* (Oxford, 1979), 'Knowledge from experience, and the problem of evil', in J. Abraham and W. Holtzer (eds.), *The Rationality of Religious Belief* (Oxford, 1987), 141–67, 'The free will defence', *Archivio de Filosofia*, 56 (1988), 585–96, and 'Does theism need a theodicy?', *Canadian Journal of Philosophy*, 18 (1988), 287–311. Phillips has restated his views in *Belief, Change and Forms of Life* (London, 1986) and in 'On not understanding God', *Archivio de Filosofia*, 56 (1988), 597–612.

examining the way in which Swinburne argues for the free will defence and the reasons why Phillips considers this to be morally insensitive, I will examine two ways in which one might respond to the charge of moral insensitivity and show why I consider these to be inadequate. I will then examine the concept of love and try to show in what sense the idea of a loving God, far from contradicting the free will defence, necessarily entails it. Finally I will see what this entails for our concept of moral sensitivity, and for the reasons why theodicy arguments often fail to offer consolation.

6.2 SWINBURNE'S THEODICY

Swinburne sets forth his theodicy in the form of a debate between a 'theodicist' and an 'antitheodicist'. The theodicist claims that it is not morally wrong for God to create or permit the various evils encountered in this world, for in doing so he provides the logically necessary conditions of greater goods. The antitheodicist denies these claims by putting forward a number of moral principles which have as consequences that a good God would not under any circumstances create or permit the evils in question.

The first moral principle put forward by the antitheodicist is that 'a creator able to do so ought to create only creatures such that necessarily they do not do evil actions'.[5] To this the theodicist replies that in a world created in accordance with this principle, there could be no humanly free agents. If we lack the ability to perform evil actions, we also lack the freedom to choose to do good: 'It is a good thing that there exist free agents, but a logically necessary consequence of their existence is that their power to choose to do evil actions may sometimes be realized. The price is worth paying, however, for the existence of agents performing free actions remains a good thing even if they sometimes do evil.'[6]

This response cannot satisfy the antitheodicist, however. Even if he were to grant that freedom of action entails the ability to perform evil actions as well as good, this cannot justify the

---

[5] Brown, *Reason and Religion*, 84.   [6] Ibid., 85.

passive evil or suffering such actions cause for others. Why
should some people suffer for the sake of others' being able to
enjoy freedom of action? The antitheodicist therefore puts
forward a second moral principle which a good and omnipotent
God should follow in the creating the world: 'A creator able to
do so ought always to ensure that any creature whom he creates
does not cause ... passive evils which hurt creatures other than
himself.'[7] Human agents would then be like men in a simulator
training to be pilots. They are able to make mistakes, but no
one, with the possible exception of the agent himself, would
suffer through those mistakes. This principle is not very
plausible for the theodicist, however. 'A world in which no one
except the agent was affected by his evil actions might be a
world in which men had freedom but it would not be a world in
which men had responsibility.'[8] The greater the responsibility
which human agents have for each other's well-being, the
greater will their ability necessarily be to make or to mar each
other, to cause each other good as well as evil. The atrocities
which people are able to perpetrate against each other in this
world merely show how great the responsibility is which the
creator has granted them for each other: 'Horrifying as the
circumstances undoubtedly are, the alternative is a world where
men have a great deal less responsibility for their fellows than
they do in our world. That men should have much responsibility
for their fellows and for the world seems in itself quite evidently
an extremely good thing.'[9]

It is clear that the fundamental premise on which Swinburne
bases his version of the free will defence, is that the freedom and
responsibility required to make human beings into moral
persons have an intrinsic value so great that a good God should
maintain them even at the price of all the evil and suffering
which human beings in fact inflict upon each other on account
of their having been given the freedom to do so. The problem is
whether the intrinsic value ascribed here to human freedom and
responsibility is as obvious as Swinburne supposes. In his
remarks on the debate between Swinburne and Phillips, John

---

[7] Ibid., 87.   [8] Ibid.   [9] Ibid., 130.

Hick admits that 'we may be tempted to feel that if morality and evil go together in this way, God should not have created moral beings.'[10] Like Swinburne, Hick thinks that we should resist this temptation. However, resisting it becomes increasingly difficult the more we ponder on the terrible atrocities which human beings are able to commit against each other. Is it not the height of moral insensitivity to think that the intrinsic value of human freedom and responsibility is by itself sufficient to justify the occurrence of inhuman atrocities in which human freedom and responsibility are flagrantly abused? If the free will defence comes to this, should we not rather agree with Phillips' conclusion that 'one of the strongest criticisms available to the antitheodicist would be the moral insensitivity of the theodicist's case'?[11]

Clearly, if the free will defence is to be maintained, it should be based on more than the supposed intrinsic value of human freedom and responsibility. It is not sufficient merely to assert with Swinburne that having freedom and responsibility is 'quite evidently an extremely good thing'. We need further grounds in order to justify bestowing such a high value on these. One way in which one might try to provide such grounds would be to argue that, although human freedom and responsibility have no intrinsic value, they do have great value as necessary conditions for real human flourishing. Human beings can only really flourish in a world in which evil and suffering are possible and in which they are free agents with great responsibility for each other's well-being and for improving the state of the world. Two further arguments put forward by Swinburne might be construed in this way.

One of these arguments[12] is that a creator who is to create humanly free agents and place them in a universe has a choice of the kind of universe to create. He can create a finished universe in which nothing needs improving, or a basically evil universe in which everything needs improvement and nothing can be improved, or a half-finished universe in which many things need improving and in which human agents may freely

---

[10] Ibid., 127.   [11] Ibid., 118.   [12] Ibid., 94.

participate in the creative process by which these improvements are to be brought about. The universe in which we live is in fact of this third kind and this, according to Swinburne, is a good thing for it gives creatures not only the 'privilege of making their own universe'[13] but also 'the privilege of developing their own characters and those of their fellows'.[14] Only in this way is real human flourishing possible. Of course, in this kind of universe it is also possible for human beings to abuse their freedom and responsibility, and thus cause downfall and suffering for themselves and others. However, this price is worth paying for the opportunity of human flourishing. Similarly, John Hick argues from his 'Irenaean' conception of the purpose of human existence in the world, that

it is not only evident why there is moral evil but also why there is natural evil. For man could not develop morally and spiritually in a paradise. The best of all possible worlds for his present comfort and pleasure might well be the worst of all possible worlds for his growth into a higher quality of existence. Moral and spiritual growth are not spontaneous but come in response to challenges, in the making of choices, in the facing of difficulties and problems, and through the experience of coping with setbacks and failure as well as enjoying success and achievement. Hence something like our present imperfect world, with its contingencies and uncertainties, is an environment more apt for person making than would be a stress-free paradise.[15]

A further argument used by Swinburne to show why a creator should grant human agents the freedom to do evil is

that various evils are logically necessary conditions for the occurrence of actions of certain especially good kinds. Thus for a man to bear his suffering cheerfully there has to be suffering for him to bear. There have to be acts which irritate for another to show tolerance of them. Likewise it is often said, acts of forgiveness, courage, self-sacrifice, compassion, overcoming temptation, etc., can only be performed if there are evils of various kinds.[16]

A world without evils would not be a world in which men could display these virtues. In such a world they would be deprived of the opportunity to show themselves at their noblest. 'For this

---

[13] Ibid., 95.   [14] Ibid., 96.   [15] Ibid., 125–6.

[16] Ibid., 90. The same point has been argued more extensively by Douglas J. Hall, *God and Human Suffering* (Minneapolis, 1986), ch. 2.

reason God might well allow some of his creatures to perform evil acts with passive evils as consequences, since these provide the opportunity for especially noble acts.'[17]

Let us recapitulate. According to this line of argument human freedom and responsibility do not have an intrinsic value, and *a fortiori* the passive evils which result from the abuse of freedom and responsibility have no intrinsic value either. What does have intrinsic value, however, is human flourishing. A loving God will therefore necessarily grant human beings the privilege of being able to flourish. This in turn presupposes a universe in which human beings have (a) the freedom and responsibility for developing their universe and their own well-being and moral character and that of their fellows, as well as (b) the opportunity to develop noble characters through the performance of especially noble and virtuous actions. Evils of various kinds will inevitably belong to such a universe, and are therefore the necessary price to pay for the possibility of human flourishing.

There are various reasons why this line of argument is both misconceived and inadequate as response to the charge of moral insensitivity. One such difficulty is the one-sided optimism with which Swinburne supposes that evil can be the occasion for good. As Phillips points out, evil could also lead to further evil rather than to begetting good.

One cannot feel remorse without having done wrong, but evil may give one an appetite for more. One cannot show forgiveness without something to forgive, but that something may destroy or prompt savage reactions. In a man's own life natural evils such as illness or social evils such as poverty may debase and destroy him... [Furthermore,] not only need evil not occasion goodness, but goodness itself may occasion evils... The depth of a man's love may lead him to kill his wife's lover or to be destroyed when the object of his love is lost to him. A man whose love was mediocre would not have done either of these things.[18]

In brief, every attempt to justify the existence of evil as the occasion for human flourishing is ill-conceived, for evil (and goodness for that matter) can easily be the occasion for human

---

[17] Brown, *Reason and Religion*, 91.   [18] Ibid., 113–14.

downfall as well. A more serious difficulty with this line of argument is the fact that it overlooks the contextual nature of concepts like flourishing and virtuous action. The specific form which human flourishing is to take, and the specific sorts of action which are to count as virtuous, depend on the sort of world in which we are living and the sort of context in which we are to act. Thus it may very well be that in a world like ours (Swinburne's 'half finished universe') human flourishing would take the form of the responsible exercise of our freedom in opposing evil and realizing good. But what about a new Jerusalem in which 'he will wipe every tear from their eyes, and there shall be an end to death, and to mourning and crying and pain; for the old order has passed away!' (Revelation 21:4)? If we were to conceive of this as a future state of the world, the way John Hick views the ultimate consummation of his Irenaean process of person making, then flourishing in that sort of world cannot take on the same form in this world, for there will be no suffering for us to overcome or evil for us to oppose. There will be no persons to make, for they will all have been made.

A similar point applies to virtuous actions. Like all actions, these are done in response to specific situations. The sorts of virtuous actions we are called upon to do are therefore relative to the situations which occasion them. In a world such as ours, a large range of the virtuous actions we are called upon to perform are occasioned by the evils and suffering which we encounter. In a different world, such as a new Jerusalem, virtue would obviously take on a different form because the situations which occasion it would be very different. Swinburne's argument seems to suggest, however, that the only sorts of virtuous actions possible are those which are occasioned by a world such as ours. It follows that if God wants us to be virtuous he must provide us with a world like this in which we can act virtuously. A similar point is made by Penelhum:

Our moral principles tell us what to do in certain sets of circumstances ... Some principles tell us what to do in bad circumstances, e.g. the rule that we should forgive injuries. In ascribing such a standard to God we do of course imply that he forgives those who commit offences against him. But do we also imply that he so prizes forgiveness in us that his goodness requires him to provide (or allow) the unpleasant occasions that call for its exercise? Granted that when Smith injures Jones, Jones ought to forgive Smith; is the evil of Smith's injury to Jones justified by the fact that only it, or something like it, could afford Jones an opportunity to show forgiveness?[19]

This argument mistakenly interprets the regrettable *occasions* for certain forms of responsible or virtuous action as the gracefully provided *opportunities* for such action. Is Phillips not correct in considering this a vulgarization of concepts like responsibility and virtue? It is as if the parable of the good Samaritan were thought to show that unlike the priest and the levite, the Samaritan did not pass by an opportunity to be virtuous and responsible![20]

Clearly this line of argument cannot rebut the charge of moral insensitivity. Nor can it deal satisfactorily with Ivan Karamazov's challenge to his brother Alyosha:

Tell me frankly, I appeal to you – answer me: imagine that it is you yourself who are erecting the edifice of human destiny with the aim of making men happy in the end, of giving them peace and contentment at last, but that to do that it is absolutely necessary, and indeed quite inevitable, to torture to death only one tiny creature, the little girl who beat her breast with her little fist, and to found the edifice on her unavenged tears – would you consent to be the architect on those conditions? Tell me and do not lie![21]

6.3 IS ALL THEODICY INVALID?

Another line of argument that is sometimes taken in response to this challenge is that of casting doubt on the validity of all theodicy as such. To the extent that theodicy is the jusification of God's ways to man, it is invalid in a double sense. First of all, it is sheer hubris from a religious point of view to take it upon ourselves as human beings to judge the morality of God's ways, let alone to decide that God's ways are morally insensitive. As Peter Geach says, 'God allows the villainy in order to have the virtue; and again it is not for us to say that he has the wrong

[19] Terence Penelhum, 'Divine goodness and the problem of evil', in M. McCord Adams and R. M. Adams (eds.), *The Problem of Evil* (Oxford, 1990), 80.
[20] Brown, *Reason and Religion*, 110. Cf. 136.
[21] Fyodor Dostoyevsky, *The Brothers Karamazov* (Harmondsworth, 1982), 287.

priorities.'[22] Furthermore, it is also logically incoherent to think that we could pass moral judgements on the ways of God. In the sense explained in sections 4.3 and 4.4 above, God's will counts for believers as the ultimate standard of goodness. This entails that it is incoherent to call God's priorities morally insensitive, since in the end it is God's priorities which determine what is to count as morally acceptable or not. Aquinas makes this point as follows:

> Were an engraver's hand itself the rule that should direct his engraving, then he could never engrave other than rightly; but just so far as the rightness of his work is measured by a rule other than the power of his hand, it is always possible that his work be done either well or not well. Now whatever the divine will does has only the divine will for its rule; for that will has no end or measure beyond itself. But each created will only acts aright so far as it conforms to the rule of God's will, which is the ultimate measure... Therefore it is only the divine will that can never go wrong; and every created will... can go wrong.[23]

Even though these arguments are true, and even though they seem to tackle the charge of moral insensitivity head on, they are not adequate for eliminating this charge altogether. True, it would be religiously impossible as well as logically incoherent for a believer to doubt the morality of God's priorities because for the believer God's priorities are the ultimate standard of morality. However, this does not make it impossible for the believer to question specific claims about what God's priorities are. Thus the believer can still question the moral acceptability of the value priorities presupposed by the free will defence, by simply denying that these priorities are in fact God's. Considering the free will defence morally insensitive does not entail ascribing moral insensitivity to God.

How can the religious believer determine whether or not the value priorities presupposed by the free will defence can be ascribed to God? If we are to accept God's will and God's priorities as our ultimate standard of goodness, then these priorities should be such that they could function as ultimate

[22] Peter Geach, *Providence and Evil* (Cambridge, 1977), 126.
[23] Aquinas, *Summa Theologiae*, 1.63.1.

standard of goodness. As we have shown in chapter 4, this entails that God should be coherent in his priorities. If God were to be capricious, continually changing his mind, approving of something one moment and disapproving of it the next, then his approval could not function as an ultimate standard of goodness. For this reason a believer must necessarily affirm that God's will remains constant. God remains consistent in what he approves and disapproves, and in this way remains faithful to his own nature or character. If we are to determine whether the value priorities presupposed by the free will defence could be ascribed to God, we will have to see whether they are coherent with God's nature or character.

It is now clear why the various attempts discussed above are inadequate to defend the free will defence against the charge of moral insensitivity. It is not enough merely to claim that the value priorities presupposed by the free will defence are in some sense obvious or intrinsic nor is it enough merely to *state* that these are God's priorities. If the free will defence is to be maintained, we will have to *show* that these priorities are not only consistent with God's will, but that they follow from his character. In brief, we will have to show that the free will defence is in some sense entailed by the fact that God is a God of love. In what sense does the believer claim that God is a God of love?

6.4 THEODICY AND THE LOVE OF GOD

Love is a relationship between persons. It follows that, if God is a God of love, then God is also a personal being who desires the existence of human persons with whom to establish relationships of love. What is the nature of such relationships and how do they differ from other sorts of relations between people?

As we argued in chapter 3, we could in theory distinguish three basic types of relation between people: manipulative relations, agreements of rights and duties, and fellowship.[24] In practice, however, human relations are usually a mixture of all

---

[24] I have also developed these distinctions elsewhere. See my paper on 'Atonement and reconciliation', in *Religious Studies* (forthcoming, 1992). For a similar distinction, see ch. 5–7 of John Macmurray, *Persons in Relation* (London, 1961).

three. Although our concrete human relations could be especially characterized by any one of these, it is rare that human beings manage to sustain any one of them in its purity for any length of time. In order to do so we would have to become either divine or completely dehumanized. Let us say something briefly about each of these relations.

First, manipulative relations. As human beings we often try to gain control over each other. In this sense Hobbes is correct in maintaining that every man is a wolf for his neighbour. To the extent that A manages to gain complete control over B, the relation between them becomes purely manipulative. In an important sense such relations are asymmetrical: only A is a personal agent, whereas B has become an object of A's manipulative power. The causal agency of A is both necessary and sufficient for establishing and maintaining the relation. In other words, A is able by himself both to bring about and to terminate the relation, whereas, to the extent that B has become an object of A's power, B loses the ability either to bring about or to prevent the relation being established or terminated.

In an important sense such relations are impersonal, because only one of the partners in the relation is a personal agent. The other has become an object. In this sense personal relations are symmetrical: both partners in the relation are free personal agents, and the free decision of both is necessary for the relation to be established. Either partner is able to terminate the relation by freely withdrawing from it, but neither is able by himself to establish or to maintain the relation, since for this the concurrence of the other partner is also necessary. (The fact that personal relations are symmetrical in *this* respect obviously does not exclude their being asymmetrical in *other* respects. In fact there are no personal relations in which the partners do not differ from each other in many ways!)

This applies to both basic types of personal relation which we distinguished in sections 3.4 and 3.5 above: agreements of rights and duties, and mutual fellowship.[25] Agreements of rights and

[25] For a similar distinction between primary and secondary relationships, see Dwight Van de Vate, *Romantic Love* (London, 1981). See also C. H. Cooley, *Social Organization* (New York, 1909).

duties are the sort of relation Rousseau had in mind in describing human relations in terms of a social contract. In such relations two persons accept certain rights and duties towards each other. Thus in an agreement between an employer and an employee, the employer accepts the duty to pay the employee a wage in exchange for the right to the work which the employee has to do for him, whereas the employee is given a right to receive wages in exchange for the duty to do some work for the employer. People usually enter into such agreements with a view to the advantage which each party can gain for himself. This is what typically distinguishes such relations from a relation of mutual fellowship in which each partner chooses to serve the interests of the other and not primarily his own. Or rather, he identifies himself with his partner by treating his partner's interests as his own. In serving these interests as his own, he loves his partner as himself. Contractual agreements between two persons can only come about if both partners freely decide to enter into the agreement. The same applies to mutual fellowship: A can offer his fellowship to B but cannot cause B to return it. On the other hand, B cannot return A's fellowship unless A has offered it to him first. In this sense all kinds of personal relations presuppose not only that both partners are personal agents, but that each acknowledges the freedom and responsibility of the other as well as his own dependence on the other for establishing and maintaining the relationship.

We can now see that if love is a relationship, it is a relation of mutual fellowship. As such, love is necessarily vulnerable. Each partner in a relationship of love is necessarily dependent on the freedom and responsibility of the other partner for establishing and for maintaining the relationship. It is logically impossible for either partner to establish or maintain the relationship by him- or herself. For most people this fact causes an unbearable dilemma. Since love requires that we give up our autonomy and acknowledge our dependence on somebody else, love threatens our sense of security. For this reason most people are tempted either to force the other or to place the other under an obligation to return their love. The result is, however, that instead of love some other relation is achieved: either a manipulative relation in which the other is forced, or an agreement of rights and duties in which the other is placed under an obligation. In both cases love is lost.

In his perceptive analysis of the concept of love, Jean-Paul Sartre explains this as follows:

The man who wants to be loved does not desire the enslavement of the beloved. He is not bent on becoming the object of passion which flows forth mechanically. He does not want to possess an automaton, and if we want to humiliate him, we need only try to persuade him that the beloved's passion is the result of a psychological determinism. The lover will then feel that both his love and his being are cheapened...If the beloved is transformed into an automaton, the lover finds himself alone.[26]

This is well illustrated in the popular song 'Paper Doll':

I'm goin' to buy a paper doll that I can call my own,
a doll that other fellows cannot steal.
And then those flirty flirty guys
with their flirty flirty eyes
will have to flirt with dollies that are real.
When I come home at night she will be waiting.
She'll be the truest doll in all the world.
I'd rather have a paper doll to call my own
than have a fickle minded real live girl.

Far from being a song of love, this is a lament on account of the absence of love! In the words of Sartre quoted above: 'If the beloved is transformed into an automaton, the lover finds himself alone.'

If God is a God of love, as believers claim, then all this applies also to the sort of relation which God wants to establish and maintain with human persons. For our present purposes two implications are especially important here. On the one hand, this means that no human person is able autonomously to enter into or to maintain a relation of love with God. For this human persons are dependent on the free acquiescence of God. In the words of Anthony Bloom,

If we could mechanically draw him into an encounter, force him to meet us, simply because we have chosen this moment to meet him,

---

[26] Jean-Paul Sartre, *Being and Nothingness* (New York, 1956), 367.

there would be no relationship and no encounter. We can do that with an image, with the imagination, or with the various idols we can put in front of us instead of God; we can do nothing of the sort with the living God, any more than we can do it with a living person. A relationship must begin and develop in mutual freedom.[27]

Furthermore, if it is true, as St Augustine argues,[28] that the chief good and eternal happiness for human persons consists in being in the love of God, then no human person is able autonomously to achieve eternal happiness. Real human flourishing is only possible through the grace of God. Augustine does add, however, that the love of God differs from the love of other people because God can be counted upon to remain faithful in his love. God's love is 'something which cannot be lost against the will'.[29] Because God is not like 'a fickle minded real live girl', Sartre's problem about the insecurity of love does not arise for the believer in the case of God's love. However, even though God's faithfulness can be *counted* upon, he should nevertheless not be *presumed* upon. It remains true that we depend on God's *free* grace in order to enter into and remain in a relation of love with God.

On the other hand, since love is a reciprocal relation, God is also dependent on the freedom and responsibility of human persons in order to enter into a loving relation with them. In creating human persons in order to love them, God necessarily assumes vulnerability in relation to them. In fact, in this relation he becomes even more vulnerable than we do, since he cannot count on the steadfastness of our love the way we can count on his steadfastness. Simone Weil explains this point as follows:

God's creative love which maintains us in existence is not merely a superabundance of generosity, it is also renunciation and sacrifice. Not only the Passion but the Creation itself is a renunciation and sacrifice on the part of God. The Passion is simply its consummation. God already voids himself of his divinity by the Creation. He takes the form of a slave, submits to necessity, abases himself. His love maintains in existence, in a free and autonomous existence, beings other than himself, beings other than the good, mediocre beings. Through love he

---

[27] Anthony Bloom, *School for Prayer* (London, 1970), 2.
[28] *De Moribus Ecclesiae Catholicae*, chs. 3 and 8.   [29] Ibid., ch. 3.

abandons them to affliction and sin. If he did not abandon them they would not exist.[30]

In other words, if God did not grant us the ability to sin and cause affliction to him and to one another, we would not have the kind of free and autonomous existence necessary to enter into a relation of love with God and with one another. Again in the words of Sartre which we quoted above: 'If the beloved is transformed into an automaton, the lover finds himself alone.'

It is now clear what this means in relation to the free will defence. Far from contradicting the value which the free will defence places upon the freedom and responsibility of human persons, the idea of a loving God necessarily entails it. In this way we can see that the free will defence is based on the love of God rather than on the supposed intrinsic value of human freedom and responsibility. Furthermore, this connection between the free will defence and the love of God sets the limits of what is being explained in the free will defence. A loving God does not desire that we cause evil and affliction to him and to each other through the abuse of our freedom. Neither should we desire it. But he does desire us to be free and autonomous and hence to have the *ability* to cause affliction to him and to each other. As Simone Weil puts it: 'It is wrong to desire affliction; it is against nature, and it is a perversion; and moreover it is the essence of affliction that it is suffered unwillingly ... But what is in fact always present, and what it is therefore always permitted to love, is the possibility of affliction.'[31] It follows that the free will defence can explain no more than the *possibility* of evil and not its *actuality*! This distinguishes the free will defence in the form put forward here from all forms of theodicy which claim that God somehow causes evil in order that good may come of it. Such forms of theodicy not only make God the author of evil and therefore a perverse God, but also claim that evil has a point. From the point of view of faith, this is a perverse claim since evil can never have a point in the eyes of a loving God. As we argued at length in chapter 3, it is *rationally impossible* for us

---

[30] Simone Weil, *Gateway to God* (London, 1974), 80. For a Jewish view resembling that of Simone Weil, see Hans Jonas, 'The concept of God after Auschwitz', *The Journal of Religion*, 67 (1987), 1–13.   [31] Weil, *Gateway to God*, 87–8.

to reject the love of God. We have every reason to accept God's offer of love and there can be no imaginable reason for turning our backs on him. The fact that we do this and become sinners is irredeemably pointless. In this sense the very question 'Why is there evil in the world?' is absurd, since it asks for the point of something which by definition cannot have a point! With reference to the love of God, the free will defence can claim that the possibility of evil has a point, but it can never provide a point for evil as such. In this way the free will defence is not affected by Ivan's challenge to his brother Alyosha which we quoted above in section 6.2. This is not one of those perverse theodicies which consider it 'absolutely necessary, and indeed quite inevitable, to torture to death only one tiny creature' in order to erect 'the edifice of human destiny with the aim of making men happy in the end'.

Does this enable us to respond adequately to the charge of moral insensitivity? Can a free will defence which is based upon the love of God be defended successfully against this charge? Let us in conclusion take another look at the problem of moral insensitivity.

6.5 MORAL INSENSITIVITY

Even if we succeed in basing the free will defence on the idea of a loving God, it remains possible for someone like Ivan Karamazov to doubt whether this kind of loving God is a good God. The price required for God to relate to us as a loving God is too high for us to pay. 'Too high a price has been placed on harmony. We cannot afford to pay so much for admission. And therefore I hasten to return my ticket of admission... It is not God that I do not accept, Alyosha. I merely most respectfully return him the ticket.'[32] Although this way of responding to the argument in our previous section does not entail the rejection of God, it does entail the claim that God should be a different kind of God in order to be good. He should be a powerful eliminator of evil rather than a loving God who is vulnerable and requires vulnerable human persons to love.

[32] Dostoyevsky, *The Brothers Karamazov*, 287.

This raised the question whether God should not be satisfied with creating 'paper dolls' whom he can effectively control and prevent from causing evil and suffering, rather than 'real live people' who have the ability to turn their backs on him. Should a good God not be powerful rather than loving? This is a question of ultimates involving a choice between two irreconcilably different ultimate 'moral universes'.[33] Since a good God is a God who cares for the ultimate good of human persons, and since these two moral universes are characterized by opposing views about what constitutes this ultimate good, they will also differ about the nature of a good God, and about what counts as moral sensitivity in such a good God.

The first of these ultimate moral universes is what we could call 'absolute negative utilitarianism'. The following argument of Karl Popper is a good example of negative utilitarianism:

All moral urgency has its basis in the urgency of suffering or pain. I suggest, for this reason, to replace the utilitarian formula 'Aim at the greatest amount of happiness for the greatest number' or briefly, 'Maximize happiness', by the formula 'The least amount of avoidable suffering for all', or briefly, 'Minimize suffering'. Such a simple formula can, I believe, be made one of the fundamental principles (admittedly not the only one) of public policy.... The promotion of happiness is in any case much less urgent than the rendering of help to those who suffer, and the attempt to prevent suffering.[34]

Here Popper defends a *limited* negative utilitarianism, whereas the negative utilitarianism presupposed in Ivan Karamazov's rejection of the free will defence is *absolute*: minimizing suffering is not merely a more practical principle of public policy than maximizing happiness, as Popper argues. On the contrary, it is absolutely of higher value than the realization of happiness – including the sort of happiness which requires a personal relationship with God. On this view a good God would necessarily be an all-powerful being who uses his power to eliminate all evil and suffering from the universe. Such a God would be morally insensitive if he should fail to realize these

---

[33] On this distinction between 'moral universes', see J. Kellenberger, 'Religious faith and Prometheus', *Philosophy*, 55 (1980), 497–507.

[34] Karl Popper, *The Open Society and Its Enemies*, 5th edn (London, 1966), I, 235. See also Ulf Görman, *A Good God* (Lund, 1977), 136ff.

values above all else. Clearly, an absolute negative utilitarian would have to agree with D. Z. Phillips in dismissing as morally insensitive the sort of God presupposed in Swinburne's arguments for the free will defence: 'If the visit to our world were by a God such as Swinburne describes, those who said that there was no room at the inn would be right. We should not be at home to such callers. And if perchance we were asked to choose between this visitor and another, we should unhesitatingly demand, "Give us Prometheus!".'[35]

The position is radically different when viewed from the point of view of the other ultimate moral universe, that is, the kind of Augustinian eudaemonism described in the previous section. As in all forms of eudaemonism, in this moral universe happiness is valued more than the absence of suffering. As distinct from other forms of eudaemonism, however, the chief good and ultimate happiness for human persons in this moral universe consists in being in the love of God. On this view a good God would necessarily be a loving God who creates free and autonomous persons even though this entails the possibility of evil and suffering resulting from the abuse of their freedom and autonomy. Such a God would be morally insensitive if he failed to respect this freedom and autonomy of human persons.

We can conclude that moral sensitivity is not an absolute concept. It is relative to the ultimate moral universe in which we choose to stand. In the end, therefore, whether or not we consider the free will defence to be morally insensitive depends on the ultimate moral universe in which we choose to stand. For those who look on life in the light of an absolute negative utilitarianism, the free will defence will necessarily be a superficial and insensitive approach to human suffering, whereas for those who interpret their lives in the light of an Augustinian eudaemonism, the free will defence is an expression of the fundamental values which give life meaning in both good days and bad.[36]

---

[35] Brown, *Reason and Religion*, 121.

[36] A similar view is suggested by Marilyn Adams in her article on 'Problems of evil: more advice to Christian philosophers', *Faith and Philosophy*, 5 (1988), 121–43. She argues that the supremely valuable good is 'a face-to-face vision of God' (136), and thinks that from this point of view an approach could be developed which uncovers

6.6 CONSOLATION

Let us finally see what these considerations entail for the claim that a theodicy cannot offer any consolation to the afflicted. Like moral sensitivity, consolation is a concept that is relative to the ultimate moral universe in which we take our stand. Which kind of considerations we experience as consoling depends directly on the moral universe in which we live. Considerations which will console a person within one moral universe may appear superficial or morally insensitive to someone who looks at life from the point of view of another moral universe, and will therefore be irritating rather than consoling.

As we argued above, an absolute negative utilitarian will consider the highest good to consist in the absence of suffering. The consolation that such a person looks for is to be found in the complete absence of suffering, or at least in the expectation that this will someday be achieved. Such a person seeks consolation from a Promethean God, and fails to find it in a world such as ours where suffering persists and where his Promethean God fails to eliminate it. Such consolation eludes us in our world, and every attempt at finding it is unsatisfactory. In the words of Iris Murdoch: 'Almost anything that consoles us is a fake.'[37] Clearly in this context a theodicy such as the free will defence, which contradicts the values of absolute negative utilitarianism, will irritate rather than provide consolation.

From the point of view of an Augustinian eudaemonism, however, the situation is quite different given the fact that the free will defence expresses the fundamental assumptions of this moral universe. Since God is a God of love, he chooses to become vulnerable in relation to us.[38] In this respect the cross of

---

'genuine continuities between theoretical and practical problems of evil' and thus offers more consolation than the 'cold and abstract comfort' (140) of the ordinary philosophical arguments. See also her 'Redemptive suffering: a Christian solution to the problem of evil', in R. Audi and W. J. Wainwright (eds.), *Rationality, Religious Belief and Moral Commitment* (Ithaca, NY, 1986), 248–67.

[37] Iris Murdoch, *The Sovereignty of Good* (London, 1970), 59.

[38] How God can *choose* to be vulnerable is shown by Marcel Sarot in 'Patripassianism, theopaschitism and the suffering of God', *Religious Studies*, 26 (1990), 366–7. For literature on the connection between love and vulnerability, see Sarot, 'Auschwitz, morality and the suffering of God', *Modern Theology*, 7 (1991), 151–2 n. 46.

Christ is for Christians the paradigmatic revelation of God's loving readiness to suffer on account of the evil that we do to him and to each other.[39] This provides a basis for believers to find consolation by experiencing their own suffering as participation in the suffering love of God. In this way Simone Weil can say that 'so long as we are not submerged in affliction, all we can do is to desire that, if it should come, it may be a participation in the Cross of Christ.'[40] Moreover, this kind of participation is mutual. If my suffering is participation in the suffering of God, then God's suffering is also participation in mine. In this way the cross of Christ provides a double consolation for believers, since it is also the paradigmatic revelation of God's sharing in human suffering. Thus for someone who looks on life from the point of view of Augustinian eudaemonism, the free will defence provides real consolation in suffering, since it expresses the fundamental values which for such a person determine the meaning of life in good days and in bad.

A theodicy argument such as the free will defence can thus only offer consolation to those who look on their life from the point of view of a moral universe of which the free will defence is a part. As we argued in section 5.5 above, it is necessary here to look on life with the 'eye of faith'. For outsiders who are unable to do so, no consolation is forthcoming here nor is any happiness offered. From their perspective both consolation and happiness have a quite different meaning. D. Z. Phillips argues similarly that

since, for many believers, love of God determines what is to count as important, there will be situations where what the believer calls 'success' will be failure in the eyes of the world, what he calls 'joy' will seem like grief, what he calls 'victory' will seem like certain defeat. So it was, Christians believe, at the Cross of Christ.[41]

But then the kind of consolation which is offered in this context, just as the kind of happiness which is striven for, are not easily

---

[39] On the cross of Christ as the paradigmatic revelation of God's suffering, see for example John R. Stott, *The Cross of Christ*, 3rd edn (Leicester, 1987), 331–2, and Henri J. M. Nouwen, Donald P. McNeill and Douglas A. Morrison, *Compassion*, 6th edn (London, 1989), 15–16, 23–4, 39.   [40] Weil, *Gateway to God*, 88.
[41] D. Z. Phillips, *Faith and Philosophical Enquiry* (London, 1970), 83.

communicable to those who do not share this moral universe. According to Helen Oppenheimer, 'it may be that Christian happiness is essentially incommunicable, because as soon as anyone reaches serenity at a particular level he or she is thereby incapacitated from talking acceptably to those who have not reached it'.[42] Before someone can be receptive to the kind of consolation that the free will defence offers, they must have been introduced to the moral universe within which it can make sense. As we argued in section 5.5 above, looking on life with the 'eye of faith' is something which requires spiritual training. If that is lacking, the free will defence remains a morally insensitive argument which offers no acceptable form of consolation.

From the pastoral point of view, the question is whether someone who is confronted with suffering is psychologically ready for the change of moral universe necessary in order to receive consolation from considerations such as the free will defence. Perhaps the free will defence can be more usefully employed in preparing people within the community of believers in times of prosperity for the day when suffering may strike them. Even then there is no guarantee that when suffering overtakes such people, they will indeed be consoled. The free will defence remains an *argument* that as such can only be intellectually convincing, which is not the same as making something your own existentially. A person may be convinced by arguments such as the free will defence of the fundamental values of Augustinian eudaemonism. Whether this intellectual insight can also be made existentially operative will only become evident when such a person actually is overcome by affliction.

D. Z. Phillips illustrates this by means of the striking example that we cited above in section 4.4. As a believer you may be convinced that the loss of a loved one will not take the meaning out of life for you, given that the meaning of your life ultimately depends only on God. But when you are suddenly confronted with the death of your own child, you may discover that you cannot put this conviction into practice. You find no support or consolation in it. The untimely death of your own child takes all

⁴² Oppenheimer, *The Hope of Happiness*, 172.

meaning out of the words about the love of God. You may still want to believe them, but you just cannot.[43]

In summary, theodicy arguments such as the free will defence can only offer consolation to people in their suffering if they have made the moral universe of which the free will defence is part, *existentially* their own. Furthermore, arguments such as this may play a role in preparing people in their times of spiritual prosperity for the bad days which may come, by awakening in them the consideration of Simone Weil, that when suffering does confront them, they might be able to experience this as participation in the cross of Christ.

[43] Phillips, *Faith and Philosophical Enquiry*, 99–100.

Theology and philosophical inquiry

What have we been doing in the foregoing chapters: philosophy or theology? It is clear that the *issues* discussed in chapters 3 to 6 are among those that are central to systematic theology: the nature of divine grace, the nature of the goodness of God, the nature of divine providential action in the world and the way in which faith can console us in affliction. These are issues which typically arise *within* the Christian faith. Dealing with them is therefore a typical example of faith seeking understanding (*fides quaerens intellectum*), and to the extent that systematic theology can be defined as the quest of faith for understanding, these issues are central to systematic theology.

On the other hand, our discussion of these issues has shown that their resolution turns in the end on the logical presuppositions and implications of a number of concepts which play a key role in human life and thought in general, and not merely in the context of religious belief: modal concepts (possibility, impossibility, necessity), relations, personhood, freedom, goodness, absolute and relative values, weakness of will, agency, the ascription of responsibility, the interpretation of experience, love, suffering, and so on. Tracing the logical presuppositions and implications of such concepts belongs typically to the task of philosophers. In this sense systematic theology as faith seeking understanding is heavily dependent on the methodological skills and the conceptual analyses of philosophers. Systematic theologians who try to dispense with philosophical analysis will have to make do with the *intuitive* grasp of these concepts, which, as we argued in chapter 1, they share with all other participants in the cultural heritage to which they were introduced on their mother's knee. In doing so they will however have to pay a heavy price in terms of conceptual clarity, methodological rigour and critical distance, and will consequently be more likely to fail in the quest for logical coherence in the proposals that they produce for conceptualizing the faith. As we argued at length in chapter 2, such failure can in no way be mitigated by an appeal to the necessarily paradoxical nature of the faith. This ploy is self-defeating, since it only succeeds in producing mystification and fails to contribute anything to the quest of faith for understanding. Clearly, if systematic theology is to be described as *fides quaerens intellectum*, it is of necessity largely a philosophical enterprise.

Largely but not wholly. As we argued in chapter 1, logical coherence is a necessary but not a sufficient criterion by which to judge the proposals of systematic theology. Philosophical theologians can therefore do no more than propose coherent conceptual *designs* for the faith. Whether such proposals are acceptable or not does not depend on their logical coherence alone, but also on whether they are (1) recognizably consonant with the religious 'cumulative tradition'[1] which constitutes the horizon of understanding of the believing community, (2) recognizably adequate for making sense of the demands of life by which the community of believers is confronted, and (3) acceptable to individual believers without their having to sacrifice their own personal integrity. In the process of reaching conclusions in systematic theology, these conditions are no less essential than that of logical coherence. Unlike the demand of logical coherence, however, these conditions are to a greater or lesser extent person-relative or relative to the community of believers. For this reason philosophers often tend to consider them irrational and consequently to underrate their importance. The result is that they often try to achieve logical coherence by means of conceptual designs for the faith which

---

[1] For this term, see Wilfred Cantwell Smith, *The Meaning and End of Religion* (London, 1978), ch. 6.

are so *revisionary* as to become morally and religiously insensitive and therefore totally unrecognizable for the community of believers. It should be remembered that the rationality to which philosophers aspire should not be limited to logical coherence but should also include communal recognizability. In the words of Stanley Cavell which we quoted in section 1.3, 'the wish and search for community are the wish and search for reason'.[2]

As we argued in chapter 1, believing, like thinking and speaking, is not a solipsistic affair but presupposes a community. The conceptual forms of the faith are shared by the community of believers. In this respect there is no more room for 'private faith' than there is for 'private language'. The conceptual designs for the faith which systematic theologians produce are meant as proposals which are presented to the community of believers. If these proposals deviate too far from the shared horizon of understanding within this community, the latter would not know what to make of them. Hence the demand that such proposals should be recognizably consonant with the tradition of faith which constitutes the horizon of understanding of the community. Clearly, then, systematic theologians should seek logical coherence while at the same time remaining sensitive to the deeper religious intentions with which the community of believers conceptualized their faith in the accepted doctrines of their tradition. This point is illustrated by our attempt in chapter 3 to conceptualize the doctrine of divine grace in a way which is logically coherent while at the same time doing full justice to the valid religious intentions of the traditional Reformed emphasis on *sola gratia*.

Of course this does not mean that systematic theology should merely repeat whatever the tradition has to say. As we argued in chapter 1, systematic theology is not merely descriptive. It has an innovative task as well. Changes in the demands of life bring about changes in the aspects of faith which are relevant and necessary in order to make sense of life and cope meaningfully with our experience of the world. It is in this regard that the metaphorical nature of religious concepts is

---

[2] Stanley Cavell, *The Claim of Reason: Wittgenstein, Scepticism, Morality, and Tragedy* (Oxford, 1979), 12.

important. Metaphors and conceptual models are selective: they highlight certain features of the faith and overlook or filter out others. Max Black explains this feature of metaphor with the following example:

Suppose I am set the task of describing a battle in words drawn as largely as possible from the vocabulary of chess. These latter terms determine a system of implications which will proceed to control my description of the battle. The enforced choice of the chess vocabulary will lead some aspects of the battle to be emphasized, others to be neglected, and all to be organized in a way that would cause much more strain in other modes of description. The chess vocabulary filters and transforms: it not only selects, it brings forward aspects of the battle that might not be seen at all through another medium.[3]

Metaphors and conceptual models enable us to notice and express certain aspects of the faith which we would otherwise have overlooked. However, they also filter out other aspects and prevent us from seeing them. At different times and in different cultural situations, systematic theology therefore requires different conceptual models in order to highlight those aspects of the faith which are relevant to the cultural and historical situation and to filter out those aspects which are not relevant to the demands with which life confronts the community of believers in the present.[4]

Sallie McFague provides a good example to illustrate this point:

In an era when evil powers were understood to be palpable principalities in contest with God for control of human beings and the cosmos, the metaphor of Christ as the victorious king and lord, crushing the evil spirits and thereby freeing the world from their control, was indeed a powerful one. In our situation, however, to envision evil as separate from human beings rather than as the outcome of human decisions and actions, and to see the solution of evil as totally a divine responsibility, would be not only irrelevant to our time and its needs but harmful to them, for that would run counter to one of the central insights of the new sensibility: the need for human

---

[3] Max Black, *Models and Metaphors* (Ithaca, NY, 1962), 41–2.
[4] For a more extended discussion of this feature of religious thinking, see my essay on 'Metaphorical thinking and systematic theology', *Nederlands Theologisch Tijdschrift*, 43 (1989), 213–28.

responsibility in a nuclear age. In other words, in order to do theology, one must in each epoch do it differently. To refuse this task is to settle for a theology appropriate to some other time than one's own.[5]

In the light of this example, the personal models which we have developed and defended in the foregoing chapters are eminently adequate in order to emphasize the agency, integrity, freedom and responsibility of human persons in response to the demands of life with which the community of believers is confronted in the present era.

This emphasis on conceptualizing the faith in a way which is relevant to the present-day demands of life is especially characteristic of what is known today as 'contextual theology'. The danger of this kind of theology is that it should intentionally or unintentionally seek relevance for the narrow context of special groups (men or women, the oppressed or the mighty, the poor or the rich, gays or heteros, specific nations or races, etc.) rather than relevance for the demands of life in our present-day inclusive context as human beings. This leads to a theology which serves group interests rather than addressing the demands of life of the community of believers as a whole. Seeking relevance at the expense of consonance with the horizon of understanding of the community of believers as a whole can become so revisionary as to be unrecognizable for the majority in the community of believers. In the end they do not know what to make of such proposals. Systematic theology should not seek relevance at the expense of recognizability, nor should it try to maintain recognizability by becoming irrelevant to the demands of life.

Coherence, recognizability and relevance are all equally essential. These criteria point to what we might call the three complementary perspectives of systematic theology: philosophical theology as the quest for logical coherence, dogmatic theology as the quest for recognizable consonance with the cumulative tradition, and contextual theology as the quest for relevance to the demands of life.[6] All three dimensions are

---

[5] Sallie McFague, *Models of God* (London, 1987), 29–30.
[6] For a somewhat similar distinction, see Charles M. Wood, *Vision and Discernment* (Atlanta, GA, 1985), 42–8.

essential. Systematic theology can be approached from any of these perspectives, but it becomes defective when it is reduced to one of these and ignores the others.

Although these three criteria are all necessary for evaluating the designs which systematic theologians produce for conceptualizing the faith, they are not sufficient to force believers to accept such designs. In the end the systematic theologian can do no more than put forward *proposals* and leave it to the individual believer to see whether he or she can accept these with integrity. Systematic theology (whether of the philosophical, the dogmatic or the contextual variety) becomes intolerably authoritarian when it claims to produce the Truth and not merely to put forward a proposal for consideration. In this respect the conclusions of systematic theology are like those of philosophy which, as Wittgenstein put it, are no more than 'samples' which others are invited to consider (see section 1.3 above). Although it is true that religious belief presupposes a community of believers, it remains up to the individual to decide whether he or she can belong to the community with integrity. The game of faith requires a community of players, but each individual must decide whether or not to participate. In section 6.6 we argued that this decision is existential and not merely intellectual. In this sense someone could be intellectually convinced of the logical coherence, consonance with tradition and theoretical adequacy of the religious framework (or 'moral universe') of which the free will defence is a part, and yet find no consolation in it since he or she is unable existentially to look on life from the point of view of this framework.

In section 1.5 we pointed out that at this level all faith is truly personal. In the words of Wilfred Cantwell Smith: 'My faith is an act that *I* make, myself, naked before God.'[7] Of course this does not exclude the possibility that others might share my personal faith by recognizing it as similar to their own. In fact all believers desire that their own personal faith might correspond to that of others in the community of believers, for only then will they be able to identify with the community without

---

[7] Smith, *The Meaning and End of Religion*, 191.

sacrificing their own personal integrity in order to do so. Nevertheless, whether somebody can appropriate a theological proposal will finally depend on whether he or she can personally accept it with integrity. This kind of 'person-relativity' applies not only to religious faith, but to all the beliefs which people hold. In this sense Augustine was right in pointing out that however much a pupil can learn from his teacher, there is one thing he must always discover for himself, that is, that what his teacher tells him is true, because no one can discern this truth for him in his stead:

If my hearer sees these things himself with his inward eye, he comes to know what I say, not as a result of my words but as a result of his own contemplation. Even when I speak what is true, it is not I who teach him. He is taught not by my words but by the things themselves which inwardly God has made manifest to him.[8]

The final words of this quotation point to another feature of the existential decision by which a believer comes to accept the perspective of faith. In section 5.5 we argued that looking on life with the eye of faith is something we have to learn. In hindsight the believer can also look on this learning process as such with the eye of faith, and ascribe it to the motivating inspiration of God. Thus faith itself is understood as a favour granted to us by the grace of God (see section 3.6 above). And therefore, *soli Deo gloria!*

[8] Augustine, *De Magistro*, 12.40, in *Augustine: Earlier Writings* (Philadelphia, PA, 1953), 96–7. See also Etienne Gilson, *The Christian Philosophy of Saint Augustine* (London, 1961), 70.

Index of names